The Easy

GREEN MOUNTAIN

WOOD PELLET GRILL

COOKBOOK

200 RECIPES FOR YOUR WOOD PELLET GRILL TO ENJOY EVERYTHING FROM APPETIZERS TO DESSERTS WITH SHOWSTOPPING BBQ DISHES

WAYNE JORGENSON

CONTENTS

INTRODUCTION

How Your Green Mountain Wood Pellet Grill Works

The name itself refers to the method of heating. Pellet grills use a different fuel to traditional grills (which rely upon sources like charcoal or gas)–they use up and burn wooden pellets. These wooden pellets look like little tablets or tiny rolled cigars; they're actually just compressed sawdust.

These wooden pellets are rotated into the fire pot, where they are exposed to intense heat, combust and emit heat and smoke of their own. This process is stoked by an internal fan, which then sends and distributes the heat throughout the grill. As you can see, this is a different method of heating–almost a combination of traditional ovens and flame cooking.

The method of cooking is called convection heating, which is the same method used by traditional smoke boxes.

The advantage of this is that the food is separated from the fire by a metal plate–which means there are no flare-ups and no grease falls into the fire pit (which can, in turn, burn up and produce an unwelcome flavor, along with being a pain to clean).

Seeing the Benefits of Your Green Mountain Wood Pellet Grill

1. Easy To Manage Temperature

One of biggest obstacles people have when it comes to grilling and smoking meats is getting the fire started and controlling the temperatures.

If folks want to use a charcoal grill then they deal with getting the charcoal lit, adjusting the vents, waiting for temperatures to stabilize, adding more fuel during a cook, etc. If they are using a gas grill then getting it lit is easy but dialing in a temperature is difficult. Gas grills are designed for Low, Medium and High. What exactly those settings means is going to depend upon your grill, the ambient weather, etc.

Dealing with temperature control is the problem that dives so many people to using electric smokers where they can just dial in a temperature, sit back and relax.

When it comes to temperature control, using a pellet smoker is just as easy as using an electric smoker! You dial in a temperature, wait 15-20 minutes for the grill to stabilize and then start grilling!

2. Flavor Is An Upgrade Over Electric And Propane

Without question, meat cooked on a pellet grill tastes better than meat cooked with an electric smoker or on a gas grill.

When you use an electric smoker the smoke flavor comes from smoldering wood chips that have to be replenished throughout the cook. When you are cooking on a pellet grill the smoke comes from the continually burning wood. The smoke from burning wood smells and tastes better than that from smoldering wood and gives a better smoke ring to boot. Same goes for meat cooked on a gas grill or smoker.

3. Minimal Flare Ups

The basic design of almost all pellet grills places shields between the flames in the fire pot and the dripping grease. This design has the intrinsic benefit of reducing flare ups to just about zero.

If you have been grilling on a cheap gas grill or directly over lit charcoal then you know that if you are not paying attention then a sudden flare up can happen and scorch whatever you are cooking.

4. Relatively Large Capacity

It doesn't cost much more money for a manufacturer to produce a large pellet grill vs a small one. The core expenses of the stand, electronics, auger, fan, smoke stack, pellet hopper, etc are constant. The only difference is making the cook chamber a little longer and the grates a little bigger.

Better to Use Your Wood Pellet Grill

1. Use Your Pellet Grill Like You Use Your Oven

One of the simplest and best tricks I have learned is to use your pellet grill like you use your oven.

Not every food is great with smoke added, but most things are! So experiment.

Any recipe that calls for roasting or baking in your kitchen oven can be transferred to your pellet smoker, simply by cooking for the same length of time and at the same temperature.

2. Use a Thermometer, Not Your Clock

Following on from the above oven tip, using a thermometer to gauge the internal temperatures of your meat will ensure a better cook rather than using time alone.

After all, it might have been cooking for the suggested time, but if it doesn't reach the right temperature inside, you could severely overcook your food. Or worse, undercook it and make yourself and your guests very ill.

Using a thermometer will also save you from opening the cooking chamber, just to keep checking on the progress of your meat.

The saying goes 'if you're looking, you ain't cooking!'. This is because as you open the door, you let all the heat escape, preventing all that hot smokey goodness from progressing the cook.

So, if your pellet smoker doesn't come with an integrated thermometer, we recommend investing in a good quality, 3rd party digital one. This way, you can monitor the cook via your thermometer and let the grill do its thing!

3.   Use Those Upper Racks

Not only do upper racks give you extra space inside your grill, but they also mean the meat you've placed on them is further from the heat source.

This means the meat is being cooked more by convection, rather than radiant heat, which offers a more even cook.

Utilize every space and rack you have, and you'll also get more bang for your buck with the wood pellets you burn, as well as have a lot more food to go around!

4.   Get Your Reverse Searing On

To sear or reverse sear? That is the question! But know that pellet grills are brilliant at reverse searing your meat, and not enough grillers do it!

To get that medium-rare finish edge to edge, with a perfectly seared smokey edge, we recommend you learn how to reverse sear.

Think of this process, almost like sous vide cooking. You create the perfect finish throughout the entire steak that you are looking for, cooking with a very low and gentle heat, to ensure none of it, not even the surface, is overcooked.

Only after reaching the perfect doneness throughout, do you then sear to create the Maillard crust and caramelized edge that creates a succulent sensory experience on top of that tender meat.

Depending on the model of your pellet grill and what you're cooking, set your grill temperature to 225f and place your meat in.

Once the internal temperature of your meat reaches 125f, which typically takes 45 minutes to an hour for a 2" thick steak (for medium-rare), take your meat out.

Crank up the grill to 500f, allowing it to heat through thoroughly, and then move the meat back into the grill, on a lower rack, and sear it for a couple of minutes with the lid closed, turning it once, until you have a great crust.

The result will be perfectly medium-rare meat throughout, with a great crust. And not a hint of that grey, overcooked outer edge you often get with the traditional sear.

5.   Creating a Smokier Flavor

This tip is for those larger cuts of meat that you want to pull more smoke into, such as beef brisket or a chuck roast.

Smoke loves cold meats, 'condensing' onto the surface more readily than it does to warm surfaces. So the colder it is, the more chance you'll give the smoke to adhere to it.

So, instead of allowing your meat to come up to room temperature – as many recipes request you to do – whip it straight out of the fridge with the dry rub you placed on it the night before and put it straight into the pellet smoker.

As usual, set it to a low smoking temperature and allow it that extra time with the smoke, to get a more pronounced smoke flavor.

Cleaning Tricks for Your Green Mountain Wood Pellet Grill

1.Burning Off the Grill after Grilling

Depends on how much gunk/food residue is left, I like to give the grill a good brush down, then fire up to max temperature for 5 minutes. Then a follow up brushing and turning off/cooling down sequence.

2. Grill Cleaning a Few Options

You can just go for a wire brush (check that you pellet grill grill can handle an abrasive brush, some can, some can't) or get a specific tool that is a bit more thorough, design specific.

TIP: If you don't have either of these tools, you can use a scrunched up bit of tin foil to clean in between the grates.

If your not into cleaning the pellet grill after each cook, a minimum of cleaning after each 40 lb of pellets should be done.

3.Ash Removal After Each Cook

Once off and cool I take the ash out, do a quick check inside to see if there is any grease build up.

Even though there won't be much, I like to always empty the ash after a cook.

Getting rid of the ash is always a good idea after each cook, and some pellet grills like the Campchef's have simple pull out knobs for ash removal.

4. Clean Probe In Pellet Grill

The internal temperature probe, once cooled, should have a wipe.

A small amount of vinegar and water, with a scourer or scrubber, is an easy technique to keep the probe clean.

BAKING RECIPES

Smoky Pimento Cheese Cornbread

Servings: 4
Cooking Time: 30 Minutes

Ingredients:
* 2 Tsp Baking Powder
* 2 Cups Buttermilk, Low Fat
* 1/2 Cup Cornmeal, Yellow
* 2 Egg
* 1 1/2 Cups Flour, All-Purpose
* 16 Oz Pimento Cheese Spread
* 2 Tbsp Bacon Cheddar Seasoning
* 1/4 Cup Sugar

Directions:
1. Supply your smoker with wood pellets and follow the start-up procedure. Preheat the grill, with the lid closed, to 350° F. Place a cast iron skillet in the grill to preheat.
2. In a bowl, mix together the eggs, buttermilk, Bacon Cheddar Seasoning, and pimento cheese spread. Add in the sugar, baking powder, cornmeal and flour. Mix until well combined.
3. With cooking gloves, carefully remove the cast iron skillet from the grill, grease it, and add the cornbread batter.
4. Grill for 25-30 minutes, or until the cornbread is golden and pulling away from the edges of the skillet.

Tarte Tatin

Servings: 6
Cooking Time: 55 Minutes

Ingredients:
* 2 Cup all-purpose flour
* 1 Teaspoon salt
* 1 Cup butter
* 5 Tablespoon cold water
* 1/4 Cup unsalted butter
* 3/4 Cup granulated sugar
* 10 Granny Smith Apples, Cut Into Wedges

Directions:
1. Supply your smoker with wood pellets and follow the start-up procedure. Preheat the grill, with the lid closed, to 350° F.
2. For the crust: Place flour and salt in a food processer and pulse to mix. Add butter a little at a time while pulsing. Once it starts to looks like cornmeal, add the water until dough start to come together. Form a round with the dough, wrap in plastic and let it cool in the refrigerator.
3. While dough cools, place a pie dish or a 10-inch round cake pan on the grill; add butter and sugar to pie dish. Let it caramelize.
4. When the sugar caramelizes and has come to a dark amber color, take off grill. Arrange apple wedges in a fan formation covering the caramel.
5. Roll the pie crust into a circle big enough to cover the pan. Prick the pie dough with a fork and cover the pan with the pie dough. Trim the crust leaving room for shrinkage.
6. Place on the grill and bake for 55 minutes until apples are soft. Let sit for 3 minutes. While pan is still hot, place a plate over pie and flip over. Grill: 350 ℉
7. Serve warm, topped with ice cream or whipped cream. Enjoy!

Butternut Squash Macaroni And Cheese

Servings: 2
Cooking Time: 50 Minutes

Ingredients:

- 1 Medium butternut squash
- 2 Cup macaroni, uncooked
- 1 Small yellow onion
- 1/2 Cup chicken broth
- 1 Cup milk
- salt
- pepper
- 1 Cup cheese, grated

Directions:

1. Supply your smoker with wood pellets and follow the start-up procedure. Preheat the grill, with the lid closed, to 225° F.

2. Puncture butternut squash with a fork several times and place on grill grate. Cook until tender, about 40 minutes to an hour. When cooked, scoop out meat and discard seeds. Grill: 225 °F

3. Cook elbow macaroni according to package instructions. Drain and set aside.

4. In a medium skillet, sauté chopped onion until fragrant and golden. Add broth, milk, salt, onions and butternut squash to a food processor. Puree until smooth and creamy. Add salt and pepper to taste.

5. Pour pureed sauce over cooked noodles and add the shredded cheese. Stir to melt the cheese and add milk to reach desired consistency. Serve warm. Enjoy!

Spiced Carrot Cake

Servings: 10
Cooking Time: 35 Minutes

Ingredients:

- 1/2 Cup Apple Sauce, Unsweetened
- 2 Tsp Baking Powder
- 1 Tsp Baking Soda
- 1 1/2 Cups Brown Sugar
- 1/2 Cup Butter, Room Temp
- 3/4 Cup Canola Oil
- 3 Cups Carrot, Grated
- 1 1/2 Tsp Cinnamon, Ground
- 2 (8-Ounce) Packages Cream Cheese, Room Temperature
- 4 Egg
- 2 Cups Flour, All-Purpose
- 1/2 Tsp Ginger, Ground
- 1/4 Tsp Nutmeg, Ground
- 1/2 Tsp Salt
- 1/2 Cup Sugar
- 3 Cups Sugar, Icing

Directions:

1. Supply your smoker with wood pellets and follow the start-up procedure. Preheat the grill, with the lid closed, to 350° F.

2. Line the bottom of 2 9-inch cake pans with parchment paper and spray the sides with cooking spray. Set aside.

3. In a large bowl, combine flour, baking powder and soda, spices and salt.

4. In a smaller bowl, combine oil, eggs, sugars, and applesauce and whisk together. Add carrots and stir until well combined.

5. Pour the wet ingredients into the dry. Stir until combined but take care not to over mix. Pour the batter evenly between the two cake pans. Bake for about 35 minutes in your Grill, rotating the cake pans halfway between the cook. Remove once a toothpick is inserted in the middle of the cake and comes out clean.

6. While the cake is cooling, prepare the frosting. Beat the cream cheese until smooth with a hand mixer. Add the butter and icing sugar and mix until fully combined.

7. On a clean plate or cake stand, place one half of the cake and top with a good layer of cream cheese frosting. Place the second half on top and cover with the remaining frosting. Icing tip: try not to lift your knife while icing. Instead make long, smooth strokes. Lifting the knife often make cause crumbs to get into your icing. Top with pecans if desired.

Irish Soda Bread

Servings: 8-12
Cooking Time: 45 Minutes

Ingredients:
- As Needed Cornmeal
- 3 1/2 Cup all-purpose flour
- 1 1/2 Teaspoon sugar
- 1 1/4 Teaspoon baking soda
- 1 Teaspoon salt
- 1 Cup buttermilk
- To Taste butter

Directions:
1. When ready to cook, set the temperature to 400F (205 C) and preheat, lid closed, for 10 to 15 minutes.
2. Lightly dust the bottom of an 8-inch (20-cm) round cake pan with cornmeal and set aside.
3. Tear off a large sheet of wax paper and lay it on your work surface.
4. Combine the flour, sugar, soda, and salt in a large sifter and sift onto the wax paper. Carefully lift up the sides of the wax paper and tip the flour mixture back into the sifter. Re-sift into a large mixing bowl.
5. Lightly flour your work surface. Make a well in the middle of the flour mixture in the bowl and pour in 1 cup (240 mL) of buttermilk. Stir with a wooden spoon. Work quickly and gently as the carbon dioxide bubbles formed when the buttermilk hits the dry ingredients will deflate, the dough will look somewhat shaggy. If the dough seems dryish, add a little more buttermilk.
6. Turn out onto the floured surface, and with floured hands, knead gently for 10 to 20 seconds - just long enough to bring the dough bits together. (It will look more like biscuit dough than bread dough.)
7. Form into a flattish round and transfer to the prepared pan. Flour a sharp knife, and deeply cut a cross in the top of the loaf all the way to the edge of the bread. Quickly get it in to bake, if it sits too long, it will deflate.
8. Bake the bread for 45 to 50 minutes, or until it is browned and the bottom of the loaf sounds hollow when rapped with your knuckles.
9. Remove the bread from the baking pan and cool on a cooling rack. Just be-fore serving, cut the loaf in half and then slice each half into thin slices.
10. Serve with butter. Wrap leftovers tightly in plastic wrap or foil. This bread makes great toast. Enjoy!

Chili Cheese Fries

Servings: 6
Cooking Time: 10 Minutes

Ingredients:
- 1 Cup Cheddar Cheese, Shredded
- 1 Cup Chili Con Carne, Prepared
- 1 Bag French Fries
- 1 Tablespoon Olive Oil

- 1 Tablespoon Sweet Heat Rub

Directions:

1. Supply your smoker with wood pellets and follow the start-up procedure. Preheat the grill, with the lid closed, to 350° F. If you're using charcoal or gas, set it up for medium high heat.

2. Bake the fries according to manufacturer's instructions. Once the fries are done, place them in a large bowl and add the olive oil and Sweet Heat Rub. Toss the fries to coat. Once everything is well coated with the oil and seasoning, spread the fries on a baking sheet.

3. Top the fries with the chili and the shredded cheddar cheese. Place the baking sheet on the grill and grill for 7-10 minutes, or until the cheese is melted and bubbly, and the chili is warm all the way through.

4. Remove the baking sheet from the grill and serve the fries immediately.

Baked Brie

Servings: 6
Cooking Time: 8 Minutes

Ingredients:

- 16 Ounce (16 oz) brie wheel
- 1/3 Cup honey
- 1/4 Cup pecans
- Crackers
- apple, sliced

Directions:

1. Supply your smoker with wood pellets and follow the start-up procedure. Preheat the grill, with the lid closed, to 350° F.

2. Line a rimmed baking sheet with a piece of parchment or aluminum foil. Using a sharp serrated knife, slice top—the white rind—off the brie. (Le the ave the rind on the sides and bottom intact.)

3. Put the brie, cut side up, on the prepared baking sheet and drizzle with the honey. Sprinkle nuts on top.

4. Bake the brie until it is soft and oozing, but not melting, 8 to 10 minutes. Let it cool for a couple of minutes and transfer to a serving plate. Grill: 350 °F

5. Serve with crackers and sliced apple wedges. Drizzle with more honey, if desired. Enjoy!

Vanilla Chocolate Bacon Cupcakes

Servings: 12
Cooking Time: 120 Minutes

Ingredients:

- 1 Lb Bacon
- 1 1/2 Tsp Baking Powder
- 1 1/2 Tsp Baking Soda
- 1 Cup Cocoa, Powder
- 2 Egg
- 1 3/4 Cups Flour
- 1 Cup Milk, Whole
- 1/2 Cup Oil
- 1 Tsp Salt
- 2 Cups Sugar
- 2 Tsp Vanilla

Directions:

1. Supply your smoker with wood pellets and follow the start-up procedure. Preheat the grill, with the lid closed, to 250° F.

2. Once your grill is preheated, place bacon strips on the grates. Smoke for 1hr-1 ½ hours or until desired crispiness is achieved.

3. Remove the bacon from the grill and set aside.

4. Increase set the temperature to 350°F and preheat.

5. Mix the rest of the ingredients in a bowl with an electric mixer until it is nice and smooth.

6. Pour the mixture into a cupcake tin.

7. Transfer the tin to your grill and bake for about 20 - 25 minutes.

8. Allow the cupcakes to cool on a wire rack. Once cooled, top with your favorite premade icing and a half of strip of the bacon. Serve and enjoy!

Pizza Bites

Servings: 6
Cooking Time: 20 Minutes

Ingredients:
- 4 1/2 Cup Bread Flour
- 1 1/2 Tablespoon sugar
- 2 Teaspoon Instant Yeast
- 2 Teaspoon kosher salt
- 3 Tablespoon extra-virgin olive oil
- 15 Fluid Ounce Water, Lukewarm
- 8 Ounce Pepperoni, sliced
- 1 Cup pizza sauce
- 1 Cup mozzarella cheese
- 1 Whole egg, for egg wash
- 1 As Needed salt

Directions:
1. For the Pizza Dough: Combine flour, sugar, salt, and yeast in food processor. Pulse 3 to 4 times until incorporated evenly. Add olive oil and water. Run food processor until mixture forms ball that rides around the bowl above the blade, about 15 seconds. Continue processing 15 seconds longer.

2. Transfer dough ball to lightly floured surface and knead once or twice by hand until smooth ball is formed. Divide dough into three even parts and place each into a 1 gallon zip top bag. Place in refrigerator and allow to rise at least one day.

3. At least two hours before baking, remove dough from refrigerator and shape into balls by gathering dough towards bottom and pinching shut. Flour well and place each one in a separate medium mixing bowl. Cover tightly with plastic wrap and allow to rise at warm room temperature until roughly doubled in volume.

4. When ready to cook, set the grill temperature to 350°F and preheat, lid closed for 15 minutes.

5. After the first rise remove the dough from the fridge and let come to room temperature. Roll dough on a flat surface. Cut dough into long strips 3" wide by 18" long.

6. Slice pepperoni into strips.

7. In a medium bowl combine the pizza sauce, mozzarella and pepperoni.

8. Spoon 1 TBSP of the pizza filling onto the pizza dough every two inches, about halfway down the length of the dough. Dip a pastry brush into the egg wash and brush around pizza filling. Fold the half side of the dough (without the pizza filling) over the other the half that contains the pizza filling.

9. Press down between each pizza bite slightly with your fingers. With a ravioli or pizza cutter, cut around each filling- creating a rectangle shape and sealing the crust in.

10. Transfer each pizza bite onto a parchment lined cookie sheet. Cover with a kitchen towel and let them rise for 30 minutes.

11. When ready to cook, preheat the grill to 350 ☒ F with the lid closed for 10-15 minutes.

12. Brush the bites with remaining egg wash, sprinkle with salt and place directly on the sheet

tray. Bake 10-15 minutes until the exterior is golden brown.

13. Remove from grill and transfer to a serving dish. Serve with extra pizza sauce for dipping and enjoy!

Strawberry Basil Daiquiri

Servings: 2
Cooking Time: 20 Minutes

Ingredients:
- 4 strawberries, stemmed
- 6 Tablespoon granulated sugar, divided
- 6 basil leaves
- 3 Ounce white rum
- 2 Ounce lime juice
- 1 Ounce Smoked Simple Syrup
- 2 fresh basil leaves, for garnish
- 2 lime slice, for garnish

Directions:
1. Supply your smoker with wood pellets and follow the start-up procedure. Preheat the grill, with the lid closed, to 375° F.
2. Cut strawberries in half and coat in 2 tablespoons granulated sugar. Place directly on grill grate and cook for 15 to 20 minutes. Remove from heat and cool. Grill: 375 ℉
3. Add 1 tablespoon granulated sugar and basil leaves to shaking tin and lightly muddle. Add strawberries and muddle again.
4. Pour in white rum, lime juice and Smoked Simple Syrup. Shake with ice.
5. Strain contents into a chilled glass and garnish with large fresh basil leaf and sliced lime. Enjoy!

Beer Bread

Servings: 4

Cooking Time: 60 Minutes

Ingredients:
- 400 g all-purpose flour
- 2 Tablespoon sugar
- 1 Tablespoon baking powder
- 1 Teaspoon salt
- 12 Ounce beer
- 2 Tablespoon honey
- 6 Tablespoon butter, melted

Directions:
1. Supply your smoker with wood pellets and follow the start-up procedure. Preheat the grill, with the lid closed, to 350° F.
2. Spray a loaf pan (9x5x3 inches) (55x12x20 cm) with nonstick cooking spray and set aside.
3. Put the flour, sugar, baking powder, and salt in a large mixing bowl. Whisk with a wire whisk to combine and aerate. Add the beer and honey and stir with a wooden spoon until the batter is just mixed. (Do not overmix.) If desired, gently stir in one or more of the optional add-ins.
4. Pour half of the melted butter in the prepared loaf pan and spoon in the batter. Pour the remainder of the butter over the top of the loaf.
5. Put the loaf pan directly on the grill grate and bake until a wooden skewer or toothpick inserted in the center of the loaf comes out clean, 50 to 60 minutes, and the bread is golden-brown. (Note: If using a glass loaf pan, the baking time might be shorter.)
6. Let the loaf cool slightly in the pan before removing from the pan. Leftovers make great toast.
7. Optional Add-ins: Bacon, cooked and crumbled, 1 cup (100 g) Grated Cheese, Red Bell Pepper and Onion, diced and sauted in Butter (1/4 cup each), Green Onions, minced, Dried

Herbs such as Dill, Rosemary, Mixed Italian Herbs, etc,.Cracked Black Pepper, Your favorite Barbecue Rub, such as Traeger's Pork and Poultry Shake, Ground Cinnamon, Dry Ranch Dressing Mix, Coarse-grained Mustard.

Focaccia

Servings: 6
Cooking Time: 40 Minutes

Ingredients:

- 1 Cup warm water (110°F to 115°F)
- 1/2 Ounce Yeast, active
- 1 Teaspoon sugar
- 2 1/2 Cup flour
- 1 Teaspoon salt
- 1/4 Cup extra-virgin olive oil
- 1 1/2 Teaspoon Italian herbs, dried
- 1/8 Teaspoon red pepper flakes
- As Needed coarse sea salt

Directions:

1. Measure the water in a glass-measuring cup. Stir in the yeast and sugar. Let rest for in a warm place. After 5 to 10 minutes, the mixture should be foamy, indicating the yeast is "alive." If it does not foam, discard it and start again.

2. Pour the water/yeast mixture in the bowl of a food processor. Add 1 cup of the flour as well as the salt and 1/4 cup of olive oil. Pulse several times to blend. Add the remaining flour, Italian herbs, and hot pepper flakes.

3. Process the dough until it's smooth and elastic and pulls away from the sides of the bowl, adding small amounts of flour or water through the feed tube if the dough is respectively too wet or too dry.

4. Let the dough rise in the covered food processor bowl in a warm place until doubled in bulk, about 1 hour5. Remove the dough from the food processor (it will deflate) and turn onto a lightly floured surface.

5. Oil two 8- to 9-inch round cake pans generously with olive oil. (Just pour a couple of glugs in and tilt the pan to spread the oil.) Divide the dough into two equal pieces, shape into disks, and put one in each prepared cake pan.

6. Oil the top of each disk with olive oil and dimple the dough with your fingertips. Sprinkle lightly with coarse salt, and if desired, additional dried Italian herbs.

7. Cover the focaccia dough with plastic wrap and let the dough rise in a warm place, about 45 minutes to an hour.

8. When ready to cook, start the smoker grill and set the temperature to 400F and preheat, lid closed, for 10 to 15 minutes.

9. Put the pans with the focaccia dough directly on the grill grate. Bake until the focaccia breads are light golden in color and baked through, 35 to 40 minutes, rotating the pans halfway through the baking time.

10. Let cool slightly before removing from the pans. Cut into wedges for serving.

Basil Margherita Pizza

Servings: 6
Cooking Time: 25 Minutes

Ingredients:

- Basil, Chopped
- 2 Cups Flour, All-Purpose
- Mozzarella Cheese, Sliced Rounds
- 1 Cup Pizza Sauce
- 1 Teaspoon Salt
- 1 Teaspoon Sugar
- 1 Tomato, Sliced

- 1 Cup Water, Warm
- 1 Teaspoon Yeast, Instant

Directions:

1. Combine the water, yeast, and sugar in a small bowl and let sit for about 5 minutes.

2. In a large bowl, stir together the flour and salt. Pour in the yeast mixture and mix until a soft dough forms. Knead for about 2 minutes. Place in an oiled bowl and cover with a cloth. Let the dough sit and rise for about 45 minutes or until the dough has doubled in size.

3. Roll out on a flat, floured surface (or on a pizza stone) until you''ve reached your desired shape and thickness.

4. Supply your smoker with wood pellets and follow the start-up procedure. Preheat the grill, with the lid closed, to 350° F.

5. On the rolled out dough, pour on the pizza sauce, cheese, and then tomatoes and basil. Place in your Grill and bake for about 25 minutes, or until the cheese is melted and slightly golden brown.

Double Vanilla Chocolate Cake

Servings: 12
Cooking Time: 40 Minutes

Ingredients:

- 1 1/2 Tsp Baking Soda
- 1/2 Cup Butter, Melted
- 1 Cup Buttermilk, Low Fat
- 1 Jar Chocolate Icing, Prepared
- 3/4 Cup Cocoa, Powder
- 1 Cup Coffee, Hot
- 2 Large Egg
- 1 3/4 Cups Flour, All-Purpose
- 3/4 Tsp Salt
- 2 Cups Sugar

- 1 Tbsp Vanilla

Directions:

1. Supply your smoker with wood pellets and follow the start-up procedure. Preheat the grill, with the lid closed, to 350° F.

2. Stir together flour, sugar, cocoa, baking soda and salt in a large bowl. Combine eggs, buttermilk, butter and coffee and mix until smooth. Add in hot coffee and stir until combined and the dough is runny.

3. Pour the batter into two prepared baking pans and bake on the top rack of your for 40 minutes, turning the pans 180 degrees halfway through.

4. Allow to cool and then frost with chocolate icing.

Onion Cheese Nachos

Servings: 6
Cooking Time: 10 Minutes

Ingredients:

- 1 Pound Beef, Ground
- 3 Cups Cheddar Cheese, Shredded
- 1 Green Bell Pepper, Diced
- 1/2 Cup Green Onion
- 1/2 Cup Red Onion, Diced
- 1 Large Bag Tortilla Chip

Directions:

1. Supply your smoker with wood pellets and follow the start-up procedure. Preheat the grill, with the lid closed, to 350° F.

2. While you're waiting, empty a large bag of nacho chips evenly onto a cast iron pan. Start loading up with toppings - cooked ground beef, red onion, red pepper, cheese, green onions. These are just the toppings we had on hand, so feel free to add anything you like! Make sure you do a couple layers of chips so everyone gets a

good serving of nachos. And don't be skimpy with the cheese - lay it on heavy!

3. Place your loaded nachos on the grill and let the hot smoke melt your toppings into one cheesy creation. Heat at 350°F for 10 minutes or until the cheese has fully melted. Remove and serve with sour-cream and salsa.

Pineapple Cake

Servings: 4
Cooking Time: 30 Minutes

Ingredients:
- 2/3 cup of vegetable oil (olive oil works great, not virgin)
- 3 eggs
- 1/3 cup brown sugar (not too sweet)
- 3/4 cup self raising plain flour
- 1/4 cup wholemeal self raising flour
- 1/3 cup saltanas
- 1/3 cup diced canned pineapple (drained)
- 1/3 cup diced raw walnuts
- 2 large carrots grated
- Icing Ingredients
- 250 grams cream cheese
- 35 grams icing sugar (not too sweet)
- Whole lemon or orange zest

Directions:
1. Mix all ingredients in a large bowl.
2. Place into 6″ greased baking tray or un-greased silicone tray.
3. Supply your smoker with wood pellets and follow the start-up procedure. Preheat the grill, with the lid closed, to 190 °F. Cook for 25-30min until golden brown and no dough when probed.
4. Let cool on rack (not directly on plate or board) then apply icing.
5. Whip icing ingredients and place in fridge until ready to coat the cake.

Mexican Black Bean Cornbread Casserole

Servings: 6
Cooking Time: 30 Minutes

Ingredients:
- 1 Lb Beef, Ground
- 1 15Oz Drained Black Beans, Can
- 1 Box Corn Muffin Mix
- 1 15Oz Enchilada Sauce, Can
- 1 Onion, Chopped
- 1 15Oz Drained Pinto Beans, Can

Directions:
1. Supply your smoker with wood pellets and follow the start-up procedure. Preheat the grill, with the lid closed, to 300° F.
2. Mix corn muffin mix according to directions.
3. Place cast iron skillet over flame broiler and heat for a few minutes, leaving Grill lid open.
4. Add onion and ground beef/sausage to skillet and break up
5. Cook until meat is done about 5 to 10 minutes.
6. Add both cans of beans, and enchilada sauce, stir to combine.
7. Bring mixture to a simmer.
8. Carefully close flame broiler and turn Grill up to 400 degrees.
9. Spread prepared corn muffin mix over top of meat and bean mixture and bake for 15 minutes until cornbread mixture is lightly browned.
10. Let sit 15 minutes before serving.

Chocolate Lava Cake With Smoked Whipped Cream

Servings: 4

Cooking Time: 45 Minutes

Ingredients:

- 1 Pint heavy whipping cream
- 9 Tablespoon Butter
- 220 G Semisweet Chocolate
- 1 1/4 Cup powdered sugar
- 2 Large eggs
- 2 egg yolk
- 6 Tablespoon flour
- 1 Tablespoon Bourbon Vanilla
- Powdered Sugar
- cocoa powder

Directions:

1. Supply your smoker with wood pellets and follow the start-up procedure. Preheat the grill, with the lid closed, to 180° F.

2. For the Smoked Whipped Cream: Add cream to a shallow, aluminum baking pan. Place the pan on the grill and smoke for 30 minutes.

3. Pour the smoked cream into a large mixing bowl and refrigerate for later use. Grill: 180 ℉

4. Increase the grill temperature to 375℉ and preheat. Grill: 375 ℉

5. Brush 4 small soufflé cups with 1 tablespoon melted butter.

6. Melt the chocolate and remaining butter in a heatproof bowl over simmering water, stir until smooth.

7. Stir in powdered sugar. Add eggs and egg yolks, stirring continuously. Whisk in flour until blended completely.

8. Pour batter into the prepared soufflé cups. Place them on the Traeger and bake for 13-14 minutes, or until the sides are set. Grill: 375 ℉

9. For the Whipped Cream: Remove the chilled smoked cream from the refrigerator, add the bourbon vanilla and whip until airy.

10. Add confectioners sugar and continue whipping until whipped cream forms stiff peaks.

11. Dust lava cakes with confectioners sugar and cocoa, top with a dollop of smoke-infused whipped cream. Enjoy!

Smoked Cheesy Alfredo Sauce

Servings: 2

Cooking Time: 40 Minutes

Ingredients:

- 1 Cup heavy cream
- 1 Stick butter
- 1 block Parmesan cheese
- 1 Sprig fresh sage
- 2 Pinch Nutmeg

Directions:

1. Supply your smoker with wood pellets and follow the start-up procedure. Preheat the grill, with the lid closed, to 180° F.

2. Pour the cream into a saucepan along with the butter and place on the Traeger grill grate to smoke along with the parmesan cheese.

3. Smoke for 30 minutes to 1 hour, depending on how much smoke flavor you want. Turn the heat on the Traeger up to 300℉ . Grill: 180 ℉

4. Shred the parmesan cheese and add it and the sage sprig into the pan with the cream and butter.

5. Whisk until the cheese has all melted and season to taste with the salt and pepper and a pinch or two of the ground nutmeg.

6. While warm, pour this sauce on anything. Enjoy!

Blueberry Pancakes

Servings: 4
Cooking Time: 10 Minutes

Ingredients:

- 2 Cups Blueberries, Fresh
- 1 Cup Pancake Mix
- 1/2 Cup Sugar
- 3/4 Cup Water, Warm

Directions:

1. Supply your smoker with wood pellets and follow the start-up procedure. Preheat the grill, with the lid closed, to 350° F.
2. Place the cast iron griddle on the grates of your grill.
3. In a large bowl, pour water, pancake mix and 1/2 cup of the blueberries and mix until combined.
4. Pour the batter onto the griddle in 4 equal parts. Cook with the lid closed for about 6 minutes, or until the edges of the pancakes are slightly cooked. Flip each pancake and continue cooking for another 4 minutes.
5. Pour the hot blueberry sauce over your freshly cooked pancakes and enjoy!

Spiced Lemon Cherry Pie

Servings: 6-8
Cooking Time: 60 Minutes

Ingredients:

- 1/2 Teaspoon Cinnamon, Ground
- 1/2 Teaspoon Cloves, Ground
- 1/2 Cup Cornstarch
- 1 Pound Frozen Sweet Dark Cherries, Thawed
- 1 Teaspoon Water (Beaten With Egg) 1 Egg
- 1 Lemon, Juice
- 1 Lemon, Zest
- 2 Prepared Store Bought Or Homemade Pie Crust
- 1 Teaspoon Hickory Honey Sea Salt Seasoning
- 1 Cup Sugar, Granulated
- 1 Teaspoon Vanilla Extract

Directions:

1. In a large bowl, mix together the thawed cherries and their juices, sugar, cornstarch, lemon zest, lemon juice, cinnamon, clove, vanilla extract and Hickory Honey Sea Salt. Allow to sit for 30 minutes.
2. Flour a work surface and roll out one of the prepared pie crusts so that it fits a 9 inch pie tin. Fill with the cherry pie filling and refrigerate. When the pie is chilled, roll out the second pie crust, brush the edge of the first pie crust with the egg mixture, top with the second pie crust, crimp the edge with a fork, and chill. Alternatively, cut the second pie crust into strips and form a lattice pattern, attaching the strips with the egg mixture. Chill the pie for 15-30 minutes, or until the dough is very cold and firm. Brush the top of the pie with the remaining egg mixture.
3. Supply your smoker with wood pellets and follow the start-up procedure. Preheat the grill, with the lid closed, to 350° F and grill for 45 minutes to 1 hour, or until the pie crust is golden and firm and the filling is bubbly. Remove from the grill and allow to cool at room temperature for at least 4 hours to set the filling, then serve and enjoy!

Baked Cheesy Parmesan Grits

Servings: 4
Cooking Time: 60 Minutes

Ingredients:

- 4 Cup chicken stock
- 3 Tablespoon butter
- 3/4 Teaspoon salt
- 1 Cup quick grits
- 1 Cup shredded cheddar cheese
- pepper
- 1/2 Cup Monterey Jack cheese, shredded
- 1/2 Cup whole milk
- 2 Large eggs

Directions:

1. Supply your smoker with wood pellets and follow the start-up procedure. Preheat the grill, with the lid closed, to 350° F.
2. Butter an 8" baking dish or a 10" cast iron pan.
3. Bring the chicken stock, butter, and salt to boil in medium saucepan. Gradually whisk in grits.
4. Reduce heat to medium and cook until mixture thickens slightly, stirring often about 8 minutes. Remove from heat.
5. Add cheeses and stir until melted. Season with pepper and salt to taste.
6. Whisk together milk and eggs in small bowl. Gradually whisk mixture into grits.
7. Pour the cheese grits into the buttered cast iron pan. Bake until grits feel firm to touch, about 1 hour. Grill: 350 ˚F
8. Remove from grill and let stand 10 minutes before serving. Enjoy!

Baked Buttermilk Biscuits

Servings: 4
Cooking Time: 15 Minutes

Ingredients:

- 2 Cup all-purpose flour
- 1/4 Cup butter
- 3/4 Cup buttermilk

Directions:

1. Supply your smoker with wood pellets and follow the start-up procedure. Preheat the grill, with the lid closed, to High heat. Spoon the flour into a measuring cup and level with a knife.
2. Put the flour into a mixing bowl. Using a pastry blender, cut the butter into the flour until the mixture resembles coarse crumbs.
3. With a fork, gently stir in just enough of the buttermilk so the dough leaves the sides of the bowl. (You may not need all the buttermilk.) For the most tender biscuits, do not overmix.
4. Lightly flour a work surface as well as your hands. Tip the dough onto the floured surface and gently bring together using your fingertips. (Re-flour your hands or the board if the dough is too sticky.) Knead two or three times, just to bring the dough together.
5. With a floured rolling pin, lightly and quickly roll the dough out to a thickness of about 1/2". Using a 1-1/2" floured cutter, cut out as many biscuits as you can. (Do not twist the cutter; push it straight down.) You can reroll the scraps if desired, but the "second string" biscuits will be tougher.
6. Transfer the biscuits to an ungreased baking sheet. Using a pastry brush, brush the tops with melted butter. Bake until golden brown, 10 to 15 minutes. Enjoy! Grill: 500 ˚F

Crème Brûlée

Servings: 2
Cooking Time: 45minutes

Ingredients:

- 1 Quart heavy whipping cream
- 1 Pieces Vanilla Bean, split and scraped
- 6 Large egg yolk
- 1 Cup sugar

Directions:

1. Supply your smoker with wood pellets and follow the start-up procedure. Preheat the grill, with the lid closed, to 325° F.

2. Pour the cream into a saucepan over medium-high heat, add the vanilla bean and the scraped seeds. Bring to a boil. Remove from the heat and allow to steep (about 15 minutes). Remove the vanilla bean from saucepan and discard.

3. In a bowl, whisk together egg yolks and 1/2 cup (100 g) of the sugar until the mix starts to lighten in color. Add the cream a little at a time, stirring continually.

4. Pour the mixture into 6 (8 oz) ramekins and place the ramekins into a large roasting pan. Pour hot water into the pan so that it comes halfway up the sides of the ramekins.

5. Place water bath pan on the grill and bake until the Crème Brûlées still jiggle in the center, about 40 to 45 minutes. Grill: 325 °F

6. Remove the ramekins from the roasting pan and refrigerate for at least 2 hours and up to 2 days.

7. To serve, let the Crème Brûlée come to temperature (about 20 minutes) before torching the tops.

8. Sprinkle the remaining 1/2 cup (100 g) sugar equally on top of each ramekin. Using a torch in a circular motion, melt the sugar until it caramelizes and forms a crispy top.

9. Allow the Crème Brûlée to sit for a few minutes before serving. Enjoy!

Rosemary Cranberry Apple Sage Stuffing

Servings: 7
Cooking Time: 45 Minutes

Ingredients:

- 10 Cups Day Old Diced Bread, Sliced Loaf
- 2 1/2 Cups Broth, Chicken
- 1 Cup Butter, Unsalted
- 1 Cup Diced Celery, Cut
- 1 1/2 Cups Fresh Cranberries
- 1 Beaten Egg
- 1 Medium Granny Smith Apple, Peel, Core And Dice
- 2 Tbsp Minced Parsley, Fresh
- 1 Tbsp Minced Rosemary, Fresh
- 2 Tbsp Roughly Chopped Sage
- Salt And Pepper
- 1 Tbsp Minced Thyme
- 2 Cups Diced Yellow Onion, Sliced

Directions:

1. Supply your smoker with wood pellets and follow the start-up procedure. Preheat the grill, with the lid closed, to 350° F.

2. Melt butter over medium heat. Add onions then celery and cook until onions start to become translucent.

3. In a large bowl, mix together bread, apples, cranberries, cooked onion and celery mixture, and fresh herbs.

4. Add half of the chicken broth to the mixture and stir.

5. Beat together eggs and the rest of the chicken broth in a small bowl. Pour into the bread mixture and stir until completely combined.

6. Add salt and pepper to taste.

7. Pour stuffing into a cast iron pan or baking dish. Cover with foil and bake on the grill for 30 minutes. Remove the foil and cook for an additional 15 minutes.

8. Serve immediately and enjoy!

Baked Potatoes & Celery Root Au Gratin

Servings: 2

Cooking Time: 60 Minutes

Ingredients:

- 5 Tablespoon butter, softened
- 2 Large leeks, white parts only, cleaned and sliced into half moons
- kosher salt
- freshly ground black pepper
- 5 Small Yukon Gold potatoes, sliced 1/4 inch thick
- 2 Whole celery root, peeled and sliced 1/4 inch thick
- 2 Cup cream
- 1 Tablespoon minced sage
- 1 Cup shredded Gruyere or other hearty Swiss cheese, divided

Directions:

1. Supply your smoker with wood pellets and follow the start-up procedure. Preheat the grill, with the lid closed, to 400° F.

2. Butter a 9x13 baking dish with 1 tablespoon of the softened butter. In a medium frying pan over medium heat, melt the remaining butter. Add the leeks and a generous pinch of salt and pepper and cook, stirring often until softened, about 5 minutes.

3. Remove from the heat and allow to cool. Place the potato and celery root slices into a large mixing bowl. Add the cream, leek mixture, minced sage, 1 teaspoon salt, 1/2 teaspoon pepper and 1 cup cheese. Stir gently to coat.

4. Arrange a layer of potato and celery root slices so they're slightly overlapping in the prepared baking dish. Repeat two more times so there are three layers of potatoes. Pour remaining cream from the bowl over the gratin, then sprinkle the top with the remaining cup of cheese.

5. Cover the dish loosely with foil and bake on the grill for 45 minutes. Remove the foil and continue baking until the top is golden and bubbly and the potatoes are tender when pierced, about 30 to 45 minutes longer. Let stand for 10 minutes before serving. Enjoy!

SEAFOOD RECIPES

Grilled Trout With Citrus & Basil

Servings: 4
Cooking Time: 10 Minutes

Ingredients:
- 6 Whole Trout
- 2 Teaspoon Blackened Saskatchewan Rub
- 10 Sprig fresh basil
- 2 Lemons, cut in half
- extra-virgin olive oil

Directions:
1. Supply your smoker with wood pellets and follow the start-up procedure. Preheat the grill, with the lid closed, to 450° F.
2. Season the center cavity of the trout with the Traeger Blackened Saskatchewan. Place two sprigs of Basil in each cavity, then add 4 lemon halves.
3. Next tie the fish closed using the Butchers twine, and then rub with olive oil.
4. Place the trout on the hot grill and cook 5 minutes on each side. Enjoy! Grill: 450 °F

Pacific Northwest Salmon

Servings: 4
Cooking Time: 75 Minutes

Ingredients:
- 1 (2-pound) half salmon fillet
- 1 batch Dill Seafood Rub
- 2 tablespoons butter, cut into 3 or 4 slices

Directions:

1. Supply your smoker with wood pellets and follow the start-up procedure. Preheat the grill, with the lid closed, to 180°F.
2. Season the salmon all over with the rub. Using your hands, work the rub into the flesh.
3. Place the salmon directly on the grill grate, skin-side down, and smoke for 1 hour.
4. Place the butter slices on the salmon, equally spaced. Increase the grill's temperature to 300°F and continue to cook until the salmon's internal temperature reaches 145°F. Remove the salmon from the grill and serve immediately.

Grilled Artichoke Cheese Salmon

Servings: 12
Cooking Time: 270 Minutes

Ingredients:
- 28 Oz Artichoke Hearts, Whole, Canned
- 1/2 Cup Breadcrumbs
- 1/2 Cup Brown Sugar
- 8 Oz Cream Cheese
- 1 Tbsp Garlic Powder
- 1 Cup Italian Cheese Blend, Shredded
- 1/4 Cup Kosher Salt
- 1 Cup Mayonnaise
- 2 Tsp Olive Oil
- 1 Tbsp Onion Powder
- 1/2 Cup Parmesan Cheese
- 2 Tbsp Parsley, Chopped
- Blackened Sriracha Rub
- 1 1/4 Lbs Salmon, Fillet, Scaled And Deboned
- Sour Cream
- 1/2 Tsp White Pepper, Ground

Directions:

1. In a small mixing bowl, whisk together the brown sugar, salt, garlic powder, onion powder, and white pepper. This will make twice the cure needed, so be sure and place the remaining half in a resealable plastic bag and save for smoking fish at a later date.

2. Lay a sheet of plastic wrap on a sheet tray and sprinkle a thin layer of the cure on it. Place the salmon skin-side down on top of the cure, then sprinkle a couple tablespoons of cure on top. Gently press the cure on top of the salmon flesh, then wrap in plastic wrap.

3. Refrigerate for 8 hours, or overnight.

4. Remove salmon from the refrigerator and wash off the cure in the sink, under cold water.

5. Blot salmon with a paper towel, then set salmon skin side on a wire rack. Dry at room temperature for two hours, or until a yellowish shimmer appears on the salmon.

6. Supply your smoker with wood pellets and follow the start-up procedure. Preheat the grill, with the lid closed, to 250° F. If using a gas, charcoal or other grill, set it to low, indirect heat.

7. Place the salmon in the upper cabinet. Smoke for 2 hours, then increase the grill temperature to 350° F to maintain a cabinet temperature of 225°F and smoke another 1 to 2 hours, until salmon reaches an internal temperature of 145° F.

8. Remove salmon from the cabinet and set aside to rest for 15 minutes, then flake apart. Reserve ½ cup to top dip after grilling.

9. While the salmon is resting, drain the artichokes, then skewer onto metal skewers (if using wooden skewers, make sure to soak in water for 1 hour prior to grilling, or you can use a grill basket as well).

10. Season with Blackened Sriracha, then set on the grill. Grill for 2 to 3 minutes, until lightly browned.

11. Remove from the grill, cool slightly, then roughly chop. Set aside.

12. In a mixing bowl, combine shredded Italian cheese, grated parmesan, breadcrumbs and parsley. Set aside.

13. Place cream cheese, mayonnaise, and sour cream in a cast iron skillet. Stir frequently, with a wooden spoon, for about 5 minutes, until the mixture is smooth.

14. Carefully fold in flaked salmon and grilled artichoke hearts, then spread breadcrumb mixture over dip.

15. Drizzle with olive oil, then close the grill lid and bake for 25 to 30 minutes, until dip begins to bubble around the edges, and cheese begins to caramelize on top.

16. Remove dip from the grill, top with reserved salmon and a pinch of parsley. Serve warm with bagel chips, crackers, or crusty bread.

Tequila & Lime Shrimp With Smoked Tomato Sauce

Servings: 4
Cooking Time: 6 Minutes

Ingredients:

- 24 to 28 jumbo shrimp, about 2lb (1kg) total, peeled and deveined
- 1 lime, quartered
- Smoked Tomato Sauce
- for the marinade
- ½ cup tequila or mezcal
- juice and zest of 1 lime
- 2 garlic cloves, peeled and roughly chopped
- ½ cup freshly squeezed orange juice

- ¼ cup extra virgin olive oil
- 2 tsp agave, light brown sugar, or low-carb substitute
- 2 tsp Mexican hot sauce, plus more
- 1½ tsp coarse salt
- 1 tsp baking soda
- 1 tsp chili powder
- ½ tsp ground cumin

Directions:

1. In a medium bowl, make the marinade by whisking together the ingredients. Whisk until the salt dissolves. Taste for seasoning, adding more hot sauce if desired.

2. Place the shrimp in a resealable plastic bag and pour the marinade over them, turning the bag several times to coat thoroughly. Refrigerate for 30 minutes.

3. Supply your smoker with wood pellets and follow the start-up procedure. Preheat the grill, with the lid closed, to 450° F.

4. Drain the shrimp and discard the marinade. Pat the shrimp dry with paper towels. Thread the shrimp on 4 bamboo skewers (preferably flat ones). Make sure all the shrimp face the same direction. Finish each skewer with a lime wedge.

5. Place the skewers on the grate and grill until the shrimp are white and opaque, about 2 to 3 minutes per side, turning once. (Don't overcook.)

6. Remove the shrimp from the grill. Serve immediately with the warm tomato sauce.

Cajun-blackened Shrimp

Servings: 4
Cooking Time: 20 Minutes

Ingredients:

- 1 pound peeled and deveined shrimp, with tails on
- 1 batch Cajun Rub
- 8 tablespoons (1 stick) butter
- ¼ cup Worcestershire sauce

Directions:

1. Supply your smoker with wood pellets and follow the start-up procedure. Preheat the grill, with the lid closed, to 450°F and place a cast-iron skillet on the grill grate. Wait about 10 minutes after your grill has reached temperature, allowing the skillet to get hot.

2. Meanwhile, season the shrimp all over with the rub.

3. When the skillet is hot, place the butter in it to melt. Once the butter melts, stir in the Worcestershire sauce.

4. Add the shrimp and gently stir to coat. Smoke-braise the shrimp for about 10 minutes per side, until opaque and cooked through. Remove the shrimp from the grill and serve immediately.

Summer Paella

Servings: 6
Cooking Time: 45 Minutes

Ingredients:

- 6 tablespoons extra-virgin olive oil, divided, plus more for drizzling
- 2 green or red bell peppers, cored, seeded, and diced
- 2 medium onions, diced
- 2 garlic cloves, slivered
- 1 (29-ounce) can tomato purée
- 1½ pounds chicken thighs
- Kosher salt
- 1½ pounds tail-on shrimp, peeled and deveined
- 1 cup dried thinly sliced chorizo sausage

- 1 tablespoon smoked paprika
- 1½ teaspoons saffron threads
- 2 quarts chicken broth
- 3½ cups white rice
- 2 (7½-ounce) cans chipotle chiles in adobo sauce
- 1½ pounds fresh clams, soaked in cold water for 15 to 20 minutes2 tablespoons chopped fresh parsley
- 2 lemons, cut into wedges, for serving

Directions:

1. Make the sofrito: On the stove top, in a saucepan over medium-low heat, combine ¼ cup of olive oil, the bell peppers, onions, and garlic, and cook for 5 minutes, or until the onions are translucent.

2. Stir in the tomato purée, reduce the heat to low, and simmer, stirring frequently, until most of the liquid has evaporated, about 30 minutes. Set aside. (Note: The sofrito can be made in advance and refrigerated.)

3. Supply your smoker with wood pellets and follow the start-up procedure. Preheat, with the lid closed, to 450°F.

4. Heat a large paella pan on the smoker and add the remaining 2 tablespoons of olive oil.

5. Add the chicken thighs, season lightly with salt, and brown for 6 to 10 minutes, then push to the outer edge of the pan.

6. Add the shrimp, season with salt, close the lid, and smoke for 3 minutes.

7. Add the sofrito, chorizo, paprika, and saffron, and stir together.

8. In a separate bowl, combine the chicken broth, uncooked rice, and 1 tablespoon of salt, stirring until well combined.

9. Add the broth-rice mixture to the paella pan, spreading it evenly over the other ingredients.

10. Close the lid and smoke for 5 minutes, then add the chipotle chiles and clams on top of the rice.

11. Close the lid and continue to smoke the paella for about 30 minutes, or until all of the liquid is absorbed.

12. Remove the pan from the grill, cover tightly with aluminum foil, and let rest off the heat for 5 minutes.

13. Drizzle with olive oil, sprinkle with the fresh parsley, and serve with the lemon wedges.

Seared Bluefin Tuna Steaks

Servings: 2

Cooking Time: 5 Minutes

Ingredients:

- 3 Whole Tuna, steak
- olive oil
- salt and pepper
- soy sauce
- Sriracha

Directions:

1. Lightly baste both sides of tuna steaks in olive oil; sprinkle sea salt and ground pepper on each side.

2. Supply your smoker with wood pellets and follow the start-up procedure. Preheat the grill, with the lid closed, to High heat.

3. Grill tuna steaks on each side for 2 to 2-1/2 minutes.

4. Remove tuna from grill and allow to cool slightly.

5. Cut into 1/2 - 3/4" pieces. Serve with a mixture of Soy Sauce and Sriracha. Enjoy!"

Garlic Blackened Salmon

Servings: 4
Cooking Time: 10 Minutes

Ingredients:

- 1 Tablespoon, Optional Cayenne Pepper
- 2 Cloves Garlic, Minced
- 2 Tablespoons Olive Oil
- 4 Tablespoons Sweet Rib Rub
- 2 Pound Salmon, Fillet, Scaled And Deboned

Directions:

1. Supply your smoker with wood pellets and follow the start-up procedure. Preheat the grill, with the lid closed, to 350° F.

2. Remove the skin from the salmon and discard. Brush the salmon on both sides with olive oil, then rub the salmon fillet with the minced garlic, cayenne pepper and Sweet Rib Rub.

3. Grill the salmon for 5 minutes on one side. Flip the salmon and then grill for another 5 minutes, or until the salmon reaches an internal temperature of 145°F. Remove from the grill and serve.

Bacon Wrapped Scallops

Servings: 8
Cooking Time: 20 Minutes

Ingredients:

- 24 jumbo deep sea diver scallops, dry-packed
- 1/2 Cup butter
- salt
- freshly ground black pepper
- 1 Clove garlic, minced
- 12 Slices thin-cut bacon, cut in half crosswise
- lemon wedges, for serving

Directions:

1. Remove the small, crescent-shaped muscle from the side of each scallop, if still attached. Dry the scallops thoroughly on paper towels, then transfer to a medium bowl.

2. Melt butter in a small saucepan, add garlic and cook for 1 minute. Let cool slightly then pour over the scallops. Season with salt and pepper and gently toss to coat.

3. Wrap a piece of bacon around each scallop and secure with a toothpick.

4. Supply your smoker with wood pellets and follow the start-up procedure. Preheat the grill, with the lid closed, to 400° F.

5. Arrange the scallops directly on the grill grate. Grill for 15 to 20 minutes, or until the scallop is opaque and the bacon has begun to crisp. If desired, you can turn the scallops on their side, bacon-side down, turning occasionally to crisp the bacon. Do not overcook. Grill: 400 ˚F

6. Transfer the scallops to a platter and serve with lemon wedges.

Dijon-smoked Halibut

Servings: 6
Cooking Time: 120 Minutes

Ingredients:

- 4 (6-ounce) halibut steaks
- ¼ cup extra-virgin olive oil
- 2 teaspoons kosher salt
- 1 teaspoon freshly ground black pepper
- ½ cup mayonnaise
- ½ cup sweet pickle relish
- ¼ cup finely chopped sweet onion
- ¼ cup chopped roasted red pepper
- ¼ cup finely chopped tomato
- ¼ cup finely chopped cucumber
- 2 tablespoons Dijon mustard

- 1 teaspoon minced garlic

Directions:

1. Rub the halibut steaks with the olive oil and season on both sides with the salt and pepper. Transfer to a plate, cover with plastic wrap, and refrigerate for 4 hours.

2. Supply your smoker with wood pellets and follow the start-up procedure. Preheat, with the lid closed, to 200°F.

3. Remove the halibut from the refrigerator and rub with the mayonnaise.

4. Put the fish directly on the grill grate, close the lid, and smoke for 2 hours, or until opaque and an instant-read thermometer inserted in the fish reads 140°F.

5. While the fish is smoking, combine the pickle relish, onion, roasted red pepper, tomato, cucumber, Dijon mustard, and garlic in a medium bowl. Refrigerate the mustard relish until ready to serve.

6. Serve the halibut steaks hot with the mustard relish.

Planked Trout With Fennel, Bacon & Orange

Servings: 4
Cooking Time: 40minutes

Ingredients:

- 4 whole trout, each about 14 to 16oz (400 to 450g), cleaned and gutted, fins removed
- coarse salt
- freshly ground black pepper
- for the filling
- 1 large navel orange
- 4 slices of thick-cut bacon, diced
- 1 large fennel bulb, trimmed, halved, decored, and diced, green fronds reserved
- 4oz (110g) baby spinach, about 6 cups
- coarse salt
- freshly ground black pepper

Directions:

1. Supply your smoker with wood pellets and follow the start-up procedure. Preheat the grill, with the lid closed, to 450° F. Place 4 cedar planks on the grate and allow them to singe slightly on both sides. Remove them from the grill and place them on a heatproof surface to cool.

2. Lower the temperature to 300°F (149°C).

3. Slice 4 thin rounds from the center of the orange and then slice each in half for 8 pieces total. Zest the remainder of the orange and set aside.

4. In a cold skillet on the stovetop over medium heat, sauté the bacon, until the fat has rendered and the bacon is golden brown, about 6 to 8 minutes, stirring frequently. Use a slotted spoon to transfer the bacon to paper towels to drain. Add the fennel to the fat in the skillet and cook until tender crisp, about 5 minutes. Add the spinach and stir until it wilts, about 1 to 2 minutes. Squeeze the juice of one of the reserved orange ends over the mixture. Add the drained bacon. Season with salt and pepper and then stir. Remove the skillet from the stovetop and set aside.

5. Rinse each trout inside and out under cold running water and pat dry with paper towels. Place three 12-inch (30.5cm) pieces of butcher's twine on each plank and place a trout on top. Season the inside of each fish with salt and pepper. Place two half-rounds of orange in each belly, rind side facing out. Top with some of the filling. Tie the trout with the butcher's twine and trim any ends. Repeat with the remaining trout.

6. Place the planks on the grate and cook the trout until they're cooked through, about 30 to 40 minutes.

7. Remove the planks from the grill and remove the twine. Top each trout with a few curls of orange zest and some reserved ·fennel fronds. Serve the trout on the planks.

Grilled Tilapia With Blistered Cherry Tomatoes

Servings: 4

Cooking Time: 15 Minutes

Ingredients:

*   1½lb (680g) tilapia fillets or other mild white fish fillets
*   chopped fresh curly or flat-leaf parsley
*   for the marinade
*   ½ cup extra virgin olive oil
*   1 garlic clove, peeled and smashed with a chef's knife
*   3 tbsp freshly squeezed lemon juice
*   1 tsp smoked paprika
*   ½ tsp coarse salt
*   ¼ tsp freshly ground black pepper
*   for the tomatoes
*   2 tbsp extra virgin olive oil
*   2 pints (1 liter) cherry tomatoes (red, yellow, or heirloom varieties)
*   coarse salt
*   freshly ground black pepper

Directions:

1. Place a cast iron skillet on the grate. Supply your smoker with wood pellets and follow the start-up procedure. Preheat the grill, with the lid closed, to 400° F.

2. In a jar with a tight-fitting lid, make the marinade by combining the ingredients. Shake the jar vigorously to emulsify the ingredients.

3. Place the fillets in a single layer in a nonreactive baking dish. Pour half the marinade over them and turn the fillets to thoroughly coat. Cover with plastic wrap and refrigerate for 15 minutes. (Refrigerate no more than 30 minutes or the acid in the marinade will begin to cook the fish.)

4. Place the olive oil in the skillet. Add the tomatoes and season with salt and pepper. Stir to coat. Cook the tomatoes until they begin to blister and collapse, about 5 minutes, stirring once or twice. Remove the skillet from the grill and transfer the tomatoes to a bowl.

5. Carefully lift each fish fillet from the marinade and let the excess drip off. Place the fillets on the grate at a slight angle to the bars. Lightly season with salt and pepper. Grill until the fish flakes easily when pressed with a fork, about 4 to 5 minutes per side, turning carefully with a thin-bladed spatula.

6. Transfer the fillets to a warmed platter. Top with some of the tomatoes. (Place the remaining tomatoes in a serving bowl.) Scatter the parsley around the platter. Drizzle some of the remaining marinade over the top. Serve immediately.

Hot-smoked Salmon

Servings: 4

Cooking Time: 180minutes

Ingredients:

*   1½lb (680g) skinless center-cut salmon fillet, preferably wild caught
*   for the brine
*   1 quart (1 liter) distilled water

- ¼ cup coarse salt
- ¼ cup light brown sugar or low-carb equivalent
- ¼ cup gin (optional)

Directions:

1. In a saucepan on the stovetop over medium-high heat, make the brine by combining the water, salt, brown sugar, and gin (if using). Bring the mixture to a boil. Stir until the salt and sugar dissolve. Remove the pan from the stovetop and let the brine cool to room temperature. Refrigerate until cool.

2. Run your fingers over the salmon fillet, feeling for bones. Remove any with kitchen tweezers or needle-nosed pliers. Rinse the salmon under cold running water. Place the salmon in a resealable plastic bag and pour the brine over it. Refrigerate for 4 to 8 hours.

3. Place a wire rack on a rimmed sheet pan. Remove the salmon from the brine and rinse under cold running water. Pat dry with paper towels and then place the salmon on the wire rack. Place the pan in a cool area with good air circulation (such as near a fan). In 2 to 4 hours, you'll notice the salmon has developed a pellicle—a kind of sticky skin or coating that will help the smoke adhere to the fish. (Don't skip this step.)

4. Supply your smoker with wood pellets and follow the start-up procedure. Preheat the grill, with the lid closed, to 150° F.

5. Place the salmon on the grate and smoke until the fish flakes easily when pressed with a fork and the internal temperature reaches 140°F (60°C), about 3 hours. If albumin (a harmless white protein) appears on top of the fillet as it smokes, gently remove it with a paper towel.

6. Remove the salmon from the grill and let rest for 10 minutes. (You can also transfer the fish to a clean wire rack and let it cool to room temperature. Cover and refrigerate if not using immediately. The salmon will keep for up to 5 days.)

7. Serve the salmon with eggs, on salads, with Mustard Caviar, or with its traditional accompaniments: cream cheese, capers, chopped hard-boiled eggs, diced red onion, and dark bread.

Honey Balsamic Salmon

Servings: 2
Cooking Time: 25 Minutes

Ingredients:
- 1 Medium salmon fillet
- Fin & Feather Rub
- 1/2 Cup balsamic vinegar
- 1 Tablespoon minced garlic
- 2 Tablespoon honey

Directions:

1. Season the fillet with the Traeger Fin & Feather Rub.

2. Make the glaze: Combine the vinegar, garlic and honey in a small saucepan. Simmer over medium heat until reduced by half. Usually 10 to 15 minutes. The glaze will be properly reduced when it coats the back of a spoon. Using a basting brush, coat the fillet with the glaze.

3. Supply your smoker with wood pellets and follow the start-up procedure. Preheat the grill, with the lid closed, to 350° F.

4. Arrange the salmon fillet on the grill grate. Grill for 25 to 30 minutes, or until the salmon is opaque and flakes easily with a fork. Grill: 350 °F

5. Transfer to a platter or plates and serve immediately. If desired, heat any remaining glaze to a boil and drizzle over top of the salmon. Enjoy!

Grilled Tuna Steaks With Lemon & Caper Butter

Servings: 4

Cooking Time: 8 Minutes

Ingredients:

- 4 tuna steaks, each about 8oz (225g) and 1 inch (2.5cm) thick
- extra virgin olive oil
- coarse salt
- freshly ground black pepper
- for the butter
- 6 tbsp unsalted butter, chilled, divided
- 1 garlic clove, peeled and minced
- 3 tbsp brined capers, drained and coarsely chopped
- 1 tbsp freshly squeezed lemon juice, plus more
- 1 tsp lemon zest
- 1 tbsp minced fresh chives or flat-leaf parsley

Directions:

1. Supply your smoker with wood pellets and follow the start-up procedure. Preheat the grill, with the lid closed, to 450° F.

2. In a small saucepan on the stovetop over medium-low heat, begin making the butter by melting 1 tablespoon of butter. (Cut the remaining butter into ½-inch (1.25cm) cubes and keep them cold.) Add the garlic and capers. Cook until the garlic is softened, about 3 minutes. Stir in the lemon juice and zest. Remove the saucepan from the heat and set aside.

3. Lightly brush the tuna steaks with olive oil. Season with salt and pepper. Place the steaks on the grate and grill until seared, about 3 to 4 minutes per side. (The tuna will be quite rare in the center, almost like sashimi. If you prefer your tuna more well done, add 4 to 6 minutes to the grilling time.)

4. Transfer the steaks to a platter and let rest for 5 minutes.

5. Reheat the butter and caper mixture over low heat. Whisk in the chilled butter one or two cubes at a time until the sauce has emulsified. Stir in the chives. Ladle the sauce over the tuna. Serve immediately.

Flavour Fire Spiced Shrimp

Servings: 2

Cooking Time: 8 Minutes

Ingredients:

- 1 pound of extra large raw whole wild shrimp
- 1 tablespoon vegetable oil
- 1 tablespoon chili powder
- 1 teaspoon garlic powder
- 1/2 teaspoon onion powder
- 1/2 teaspoon cayenne pepper
- 1/4 teaspoon paprika
- 1/4 teaspoon dried oregano
- Pinch of Kosher salt

Directions:

1. Supply your smoker with wood pellets and follow the start-up procedure. Preheat the grill, with the lid closed, to High heat.

2. While grill is preheating, remove the shrimp shells, leaving the heads.

3. Butterfly shrimp by using a knife to cut each shrimp down the middle, from the head down to the tail.

4. Remove the vein, rinse off the shrimp and lightly dry off with paper towels.

5. Place the shrimp in a large bowl, sprinkle with all the seasonings and the oil.

6. Mix together, ensuring the mixture evenly covers each shrimp.

7. Using a skewer, impale the whole body of a shrimp, from head to tail. (Wrap them in aluminum foil if using wooden skewers).

8. Place the whole shrimp on the grill and cook for 3-4 minutes on each side (Or until shells turns pink and the shrimp is opaque).

9. Serve with your favorite sauce or condiment.

Moules Marinières With Garlic Butter Sauce

Servings: 4
Cooking Time: 12 Minutes

Ingredients:

- 3lb (1.4kg) fresh mussels, scrubbed under cold running water and debearded
- lemon wedges
- crusty bread (optional)
- for the sauce
- 6 tbsp unsalted butter
- 3 garlic cloves, peeled and minced
- 1 cup dry white wine or hard cider
- 1 tbsp freshly squeezed lemon juice
- 2 tsp hot sauce, plus more
- coarse salt
- freshly ground black pepper
- 2 tbsp chopped fresh curly parsley or tarragon

Directions:

1. Supply your smoker with wood pellets and follow the start-up procedure. Preheat the grill, with the lid closed, to 450° F.

2. In a small saucepan on the stovetop over medium-low heat, make the sauce by melting the butter. Add the garlic and sauté for 1 to 2 minutes. Add the wine, lemon juice, and hot sauce. Season with salt and pepper to taste. Simmer for 5 minutes. Remove the saucepan from the heat and stir in the parsley. Keep warm.

3. Discard any mussels that are cracked or don't snap shut when tapped. Place the mussels in a large aluminum foil roasting pan and cover tightly with heavy-duty aluminum foil.

4. Place the pan on the grate and steam the mussels until the shells open, about 10 to 12 minutes. Remove the pan from the grill and use long-handled tongs to remove the foil from the pan. (Be careful of escaping steam.) Use the tongs to discard any mussels that don't open.

5. Pour the reserved garlic butter sauce over the mussels. Serve from the pan or transfer the mussels to a shallow serving bowl. Serve immediately with lemon wedges, additional hot sauce, and crusty bread (if using) to sop up the juices.

Smoked Fish Chowder

Servings: 4
Cooking Time: 60 Minutes

Ingredients:

- 12 Ounce (1-1/2 to 2 lb) skin-on salmon fillet, preferably wild-caught
- Fin & Feather Rub
- 2 Corn Husks
- 3 Slices Bacon, sliced
- 4 Can Cream of Potato Soup, Condensed
- 3 Cup whole milk
- 8 Ounce cream cheese
- 3 green onions, thinly sliced
- 2 Teaspoon hot sauce

Directions:

1. Supply your smoker with wood pellets and follow the start-up procedure. Preheat the grill, with the lid closed, to 180° F.

2. Sprinkle Traeger Fin & Feather rub as needed on salmon. Arrange the salmon skin-side down on the grill grate. Smoke for 30 minutes. Grill: 180 °F

3. Increase the grill temperature to 350°F. Grill: 350 °F

4. Cook the salmon for 30 minutes, or until the fish flakes easily with a fork. (The exact time will depend on the thickness of the fillet.) There is no need to turn the fish. Using a large thin spatula, transfer the salmon to a wire rack to cool. Remove the skin. (The salmon can be made a day ahead, wrapped in plastic wrap and refrigerated.) Break into flakes and set aside.

5. Arrange the corn and bacon strips on the grill grate. (The salmon will be roasting while you do this.) Roast the corn and the bacon until the corn is cooked through and browned in spots, turning as needed, and the bacon is crisp, about 15 minutes.

6. In the meantime, bring the cream of potato soup and the milk to a simmer over medium heat in a large saucepan or Dutch oven on the stovetop. Gradually stir in the cream cheese and whisk to blend. Chop the bacon into bits and slice the corn off the cobs using long strokes of a chef's knife.

7. Add to the soup along with the green onions. Stir in the salmon. Heat gently for 5 to 10 minutes. Add the hot sauce to taste. If the chowder is too thick, add more milk. Serve at once. Enjoy!

Roasted Halibut With Spring Vegetables

Servings: 4
Cooking Time: 20 Minutes
Ingredients:

- 4 thick-cut halibut fillets
- 2 Tablespoon Fin & Feather Rub
- Butcher Paper
- 1 Pound Carrots, Peeled and Cut into 3/4" Inch Slices
- 1 Pound asparagus, ends trimmed
- 1/2 Pound Oyster Mushrooms
- 2 Tablespoon butter
- salt and pepper
- 1/2 Cup white wine

Directions:
1. Season the halibut fillets with Traeger Fin and Feather Rub.

2. To build the packets: Start with four sheets of parchment paper about twenty inches long. Fold in half, then open it back up.

3. Divide the carrots, asparagus, and mushrooms between the four pieces of parchment and top each with a little bit of butter. Season with salt and pepper. Place a halibut fillet on top of the vegetables in each packet.

4. Next, fold the paper over so the two ends meet, enclosing the food. Beginning at either end of the center crease, make small, overlapping diagonal folds around the filling, sealing the packet tight. Before finishing the final fold, pour a little bit of wine in each packet then seal completely.

5. Supply your smoker with wood pellets and follow the start-up procedure. Preheat the grill, with the lid closed, to 500° F.

6. Place all four packets on a sheet tray and place in the grill. Cook for 7-10 minutes or until the internal temperature of the fish reaches 145°F. Remove from the grill and place packet on a serving dish. Grill: 500 °F Probe: 145 °F

7. Using a knife or scissors, cut open each packet and fold the edges back. Finish with a little bit of lemon juice if desired. Enjoy!

Lobster Tail

Servings: 2

Cooking Time: 25 Minutes

Ingredients:

- 2 lobster tails
- Salt
- Freshly ground black pepper
- 1 batch Lemon Butter Mop for Seafood

Directions:

1. Supply your smoker with wood pellets and follow the start-up procedure. Preheat the grill, with the lid closed, to 375°F.

2. Using kitchen shears, slit the top of the lobster shells, through the center, nearly to the tail. Once cut, expose as much meat as you can through the cut shell.

3. Season the lobster tails all over with salt and pepper.

4. Place the tails directly on the grill grate and grill until their internal temperature reaches 145°F. Remove the lobster from the grill and serve with the mop on the side for dipping.

Seared Ahi Tuna Steak With Soy Sauce

Servings: 2

Cooking Time: 60 Minutes

Ingredients:

- 1/2 Cup Gluten Free Soy Sauce
- 1 Large Sushi Grade Ahi Tuna Steak, Patted Dry
- 1/4 Cup Lime Juice
- 2 Tablespoons Rice Wine Vinegar
- 2 Tablespoons Sesame Oil, Divided
- 2 Tablespoons Sriracha Sauce
- 4 Tablespoons Sweet Heat Rub
- 2 Cups Water

Directions:

1. Supply your smoker with wood pellets and follow the start-up procedure. Preheat the grill, with the lid closed, to 400° F. If using gas or charcoal, set it up for high heat over direct heat.

2. In the glass baking dish, pour in the water, soy sauce, lime juice, rice wine vinegar, 1 tablespoon sesame oil, sriracha sauce, and mirin. Whisk the marinade together with the whisk until everything is well combine. Place the ahi steak into the marinade and place the glass baking dish with the ahi steak in the refrigerator for 30 minutes. After 30 minutes, flip the ahi steak over so that the ahi has the chance to fully marinate on all sides, and allow to marinate for 30 more minutes.

3. After the tuna steak has finished marinating, drain off the marinade and pat the steak dry with paper towels on all sides. Pour the Sweet Heat Rub onto the plate and rub the remaining tablespoon of sesame oil generously on all sides of the tuna steak, and then gently place the tuna steak into the seasoning on the plate, turning on all sides to coat evenly.

4. Insert a temperature probe into the thickest part of the ahi steak and place the steak on the hottest part of the grill. Grill the ahi tuna steak for 45 seconds on each side, or just until the outside is opaque and has grill marks. Flip the steak and allow it to grill for another 45 seconds until the outside is just cooked through. The ahi tuna steak's internal temperature should be just at 115°F.

5. Remove the steak from the grill once it reaches 115°F, and immediately slice and serve. The inside of the steak should still be cool and ruby pink.

Mexican Mahi Mahi With Baja Cabbage Slaw

Servings: 4

Cooking Time: 10 Minutes

Ingredients:

- 1½lb (680g) skinless mahi mahi, cod, or other firm white fish fillets
- coarse salt
- freshly ground black pepper
- chili powder
- lime wedges
- for the slaw
- 2 cups finely shredded green cabbage
- 2 cups finely shredded purple cabbage
- 4 tbsp reduced-fat mayo
- 2 tsp hot sauce, plus more
- 2 tsp freshly squeezed lime juice
- ½ tsp coarse salt
- for the marinade
- ¼ cup freshly squeezed orange juice
- ¼ cup freshly squeezed lime juice
- 2 tbsp extra virgin olive oil

Directions:

1. In a medium bowl, make the slaw by combining the ingredients. Stir well. Transfer to a serving bowl. Cover and refrigerate until ready to serve.

2. Place the fish fillets in a baking dish and pour the orange and lime juices and olive oil over them. Turn the fillets to coat thoroughly. Cover and refrigerate for 15 to 20 minutes.

3. Supply your smoker with wood pellets and follow the start-up procedure. Preheat the grill, with the lid closed, to 450° F.

4. Drain the fish and pat dry with paper towels. (Discard the marinade.) Season the fillets on both sides with salt and pepper and chili powder. Place the fillets on the grate and grill until golden brown, about 4 to 5 minutes per side, turning with a thin-bladed spatula.

5. Transfer the fish to a platter. Serve with the slaw and lime wedges.

Smoked Sugar Halibut

Servings: 8

Cooking Time: 120 Minutes

Ingredients:

- 1/4 cup granulated sugar
- 1/4 cup brown sugar
- 1/2 cup kosher salt
- 1 tsp ground coriander
- 2 lbs fresh halibut

Directions:

1. In a small bowl, mix the sugars, salt, and coriander together. Season the halibut on all sides.

2. Wrap the halibut in plastic wrap, place on a rimmed sheet pan, and brine in the fridge for 3 hours.

3. Remove the plastic wrap and rinse the fish. Pat it dry. Set it on a drying rack over a sheet pan for 1-2 hours in the fridge.

4. Supply your smoker with wood pellets and follow the start-up procedure. Preheat the grill, with the lid closed, to 200° F. Smoke the fish for 2 hours or until its internal temperature reaches 140 °F.

5. Serve your preferred sauce with the fish.

Kimi's Simple Grilled Fresh Fish

Servings: 2

Cooking Time: 45 Minutes

Ingredients:

- 1 Cup soy sauce
- 1/3 Cup extra-virgin olive oil
- 1 Tablespoon garlic, minced
- 2 lemons, juiced
- fresh basil
- 4 Pound Fresh Fish, cut into portion-sized pieces

Directions:

1. Mix all ingredients to create sauce and cover fish in marinade for 45 minutes.

2. Supply your smoker with wood pellets and follow the start-up procedure. Preheat the grill, with the lid closed, to 140° F. Grill the marinated fish on the grill until it reaches an internal temperature of 140-145℉. Serve immediately, enjoy! Grill: 350 ℉ Probe: 145 ℉

Traeger Crab Legs

Servings: 4

Cooking Time: 30 Minutes

Ingredients:

- 3 Pound crab legs, thawed and halved
- 1 Cup butter, melted
- 2 Tablespoon fresh lemon juice
- 2 Clove garlic, minced
- 1 Tablespoon Fin & Feather Rub or Old Bay Seasoning, plus more to taste
- lemon wedges
- Italian Parsley, chopped

Directions:

1. If the crab legs are too long to fit in the roasting pan, break them down at the joints by twisting, or use a heavy knife or cleaver. Split the shells open lengthwise. Transfer to the roasting pan.

2. Combine the butter, lemon juice and garlic; whisk to mix. Pour mixture over the crab legs, turning the legs to coat. Sprinkle the Traeger Fin & Feather Rub or Old Bay Seasoning over the legs.

3. Supply your smoker with wood pellets and follow the start-up procedure. Preheat the grill, with the lid closed, to 350° F.

4. Cook the crab legs, basting once or twice with the butter sauce from the bottom of the pan, for 20 to 30 minutes (depending on the size of the crab legs) or until warmed through. Grill: 350 ℉

5. Transfer the crab legs to a large platter and divide the sauce and accumulated juices between 4 dipping bowls. Enjoy!

Grilled Oysters With Mignonette

Servings: 2

Cooking Time: 15 Minutes

Ingredients:

- 4 Cup rock salt
- 18 Large oysters
- 4 Tablespoon unsalted butter
- 2 Clove garlic, minced
- kosher salt
- 12 Medium lemon wedges, for serving
- 2 Tablespoon minced shallot
- 1/4 Cup red wine vinegar
- 1/2 Teaspoon freshly ground black pepper

Directions:

1. Choose a shallow serving platter that will hold all of the oysters. Pour the rock salt onto the platter to create a 1/2 inch base. This will steady the oysters for serving.

2. To prepare the oysters, check to ensure they are completely closed. Discard oysters that are not. Wash and lightly scrub the oysters to ensure there is no grit on the surface. This will prevent the grit from entering the oyster once shucked.

3. Using a thick glove or kitchen towel, sturdy the oyster in the hand opposite of the one holding the knife. Using an oyster knife or very sturdy paring knife, locate the "hinge" on each oyster. Place the point of the knife in the hinge, and wiggle the tip of the knife into the oyster until it feels sturdy. Firmly turn the knife to apply a torquing pressure to gently open the oyster.

4. Remove the top shell of the oyster. Using the tip of the knife, loosen the oyster from its shell, leaving the juices intact. Place each loosened oyster on its half shell on a baking sheet.

5. Supply your smoker with wood pellets and follow the start-up procedure. Preheat the grill, with the lid closed, to 450° F.

6. In a small saucepan, melt the butter over medium-low heat. Add the garlic and a generous pinch of salt, and cook until fragrant but not burned, about 1 minute. Remove from the heat. Grill: 450 ℉

7. For the Mignonette: Combine the minced shallot, red wine vinegar and 1/2 teaspoon freshly ground black pepper. Set aside.

8. Spoon 1 teaspoon of the garlic butter sauce onto each oyster in its half shell. Carefully place each oyster directly on the grill grates, ensuring they don't slip. Close the lid and allow them to cook for 3 to 4 minutes, until the edges of the oysters have pulled away from the shell. Remove carefully with tongs to keep the juices and butter in the shells. Place directly on the rock salt to balance them. Serve immediately with the mignonette and lemon wedges to squeeze onto the oysters. Enjoy!

VEGETABLES RECIPES

Whole Roasted Cauliflower With Garlic Parmesan Butter

Servings: 4
Cooking Time: 45 Minutes

Ingredients:
- 1 Whole head cauliflower
- 1/4 Cup olive oil
- salt and pepper
- 1/2 Cup butter, melted
- 1/4 Cup shredded Parmesan cheese
- 2 Clove garlic, minced
- 1/2 Tablespoon chopped parsley

Directions:

1. Supply your smoker with wood pellets and follow the start-up procedure. Preheat the grill, with the lid closed, to 450° F.

2. Brush the cauliflower with olive oil and season liberally with salt and pepper.

3. Put cauliflower in a cast iron skillet, place directly on the grill grate and cook for 45 minutes until golden brown and the center is tender.

4. While the cauliflower is cooking, combine the melted butter, parmesan, garlic and parsley in a small bowl.

5. During the last 20 minutes of cooking, baste the cauliflower with the melted butter mixture.

6. Remove the cauliflower from the grill and top with extra parmesan and parsley if desired. Enjoy!

Baked Sweet And Savory Yams By Bennie Kendrick

Servings: 6
Cooking Time: 60 Minutes

Ingredients:
- 3 Medium Yams
- 3 Tablespoon extra-virgin olive oil
- honey
- Goat Cheese
- 1/2 Cup brown sugar
- 1/2 Cup Pecans, pieces

Directions:

1. Supply your smoker with wood pellets and follow the start-up procedure. Preheat the grill, with the lid closed, to 350° F.

2. While Traeger comes to temperature, wash yams and poke a few holes all over. Wrap yams in foil.

3. Bake for 45-60 minutes or until knife tender. You don't want to overcook and get the yams too soft because you want to be able to cut each yam into rounds.

4. Once yams have cooled to the touch, cut each into 1/4" rounds. Lightly coat each round with oil olive and place on sheet tray.

5. Sprinkle each top with brown sugar. Using a teaspoon, place desired amount of goat cheese on each round. Next top with chopped pecans. Finally, drizzle Bee Local honey over each round.

6. Based on how sweet you like your yams, you can add more brown sugar and honey.

7. After complete, place your sheet tray back in the grill and cook, lid closed, for another 20 minutes. Enjoy!

Grilled Beer Cabbage

Servings: 4

Cooking Time: 50 Minutes

Ingredients:

- 2 Cabbage, head
- 1 Tablespoon extra-virgin olive oil
- 1 Teaspoon salt
- 1 Teaspoon freshly ground black pepper
- 14 Fluid Ounce Guinness Extra Stout

Directions:

1. Clean and core cabbages. Drizzle with olive oil and salt and pepper. Rub into the cabbage.

2. Supply your smoker with wood pellets and follow the start-up procedure. Preheat the grill, with the lid closed, to 180° F.

3. Place cabbages directly on grill grate; smoke for 15 to 20 minutes. Remove from grill and thickly slice cabbage. Grill: 180 °F

4. Place sliced cabbage in cast-iron skillet. Pour beer over cabbage and return to grill.

5. Increase temperature to 375°F and cook for 30 minutes, or until cabbage has reached desired softness. Grill: 375 °F

6. Serve with corned beef. Enjoy!

Roasted Green Beans With Bacon

Servings: 4

Cooking Time: 20 Minutes

Ingredients:

- 1 1/2 Pound green beans, ends trimmed
- 4 Strips bacon, cut into small pieces
- 4 Tablespoon extra-virgin olive oil
- 2 Clove garlic, minced
- 1 Teaspoon kosher salt

Directions:

1. Supply your smoker with wood pellets and follow the start-up procedure. Preheat the grill, with the lid closed, to 350° F.

2. Toss all ingredients together and spread out evenly on a sheet tray.

3. Place the tray directly on the grill grate and roast until the bacon is crispy and beans are lightly browned, about 20 minutes. Enjoy! Grill: 450 °F

Roasted Sheet Pan Vegetables

Servings: 4

Cooking Time: 25 Minutes

Ingredients:

- 1 Small head purple cauliflower, stemmed and cut into 2 inch florets
- 1 Small head yellow cauliflower, stemmed and cut into 2 inch florets
- 4 Cup butternut squash
- 2 Cup oyster or shiitake mushrooms, rinsed and sliced
- 3 Tablespoon olive oil
- 2 Teaspoon kosher salt
- freshly ground black pepper
- 1/4 Cup chopped flat-leaf parsley

Directions:

1. Supply your smoker with wood pellets and follow the start-up procedure. Preheat the grill, with the lid closed, to 450° F.

2. In a large mixing bowl, combine all of the vegetables. Drizzle olive oil over the top, along with kosher salt and a generous grinding of black pepper.

3. Using your hands, toss the vegetables until they are evenly coated.

4. Spread out onto 1 or 2 half sheet pans or baking sheets, ensuring there is a little space

between the veggies. (If they are too crowded, the vegetables will steam instead of roast and you won't get that crispy texture.)

5. Place the sheet pans on the grill and cook for 15 minutes. Open and stir, then close the lid and continue to cook until the vegetables are brown around the edges, about 5 to 15 minutes longer. Grill: 450 °F

6. Toss with parsley and serve immediately. The vegetables are also delicious at room temperature. Enjoy!

Portobello Marinated Mushroom

Servings: 2
Cooking Time: 15 Minutes

Ingredients:

- 1 Teaspoon chopped thyme
- 1 Teaspoon rosemary, chopped
- 1 Teaspoon Oregano, chopped
- 3 Tablespoon extra-virgin olive oil
- 1 To Taste Jacobsen Salt Co. Pure Kosher Sea Salt
- 1 To Taste pepper
- 6 Whole Portobello Mushroom
- 2 Whole russet potatoes

Directions:

1. Supply your smoker with wood pellets and follow the start-up procedure. Preheat the grill, with the lid closed, to 450° F.

2. Mix fresh herbs, olive oil, salt, and pepper together in a bowl. Rub over mushrooms. Grill both sides of mushrooms for approximately 2-3 minutes on each side. Grill: 450 °F

3. Clean the potatoes and slice into long strips.

4. Heat the oil on the Traeger in a sauce pan; drop the potatoes in the hot oil and fry for 7-8 minutes. Let the potatoes cool slightly on a sheet pan. Enjoy! Grill: 450 °F

Christmas Brussel Sprouts

Servings: 6
Cooking Time: 50 Minutes

Ingredients:

- 1/2 Pound thick-cut bacon
- 1 Medium onion, diced
- 2 Pound fresh Brussels sprouts
- 2 Tablespoon olive oil
- salt and pepper

Directions:

1. Supply your smoker with wood pellets and follow the start-up procedure. Preheat the grill, with the lid closed, to 350° F.

2. Place bacon directly on grill grate and cook for 15-20 minutes, or until lightly browned. Remove from grill and set aside on paper towel lined plate.

3. Slice onion in half and then slice into 1/4 inch moons and add to large mixing bowl. Slice brussels sprouts in half lengthwise and add to bowl.

4. Cut reserved bacon into 1/2 inch pieces and add to bowl. Drizzle with olive oil and sprinkle with salt and pepper. Toss to coat and pour into baking pan.

5. Turn the temperature on grill to 375 and place baking pan on grill. Roast for 30 minutes mixing halfway through cooking. Grill: 375 °F

Butternut Squash

Servings: 4

Cooking Time: 45 Minutes

Ingredients:

- 1 Whole butternut squash
- Veggie Rub
- Blackened Saskatchewan Rub
- olive oil

Directions:

1. Cut squash in half and lightly coat with mixture of olive oil, Traeger Veggie Shake, and Traeger Blackened Saskatchewan.

2. Wrap in foil with 1/2 cup (120mL) of water.

3. Supply your smoker with wood pellets and follow the start-up procedure. Preheat the grill, with the lid closed, to 450° F.

4. Place squash on grill for 45 minutes. Remove from grill and unwrap. Enjoy!

Blt Pasta Salad

Servings: 6

Cooking Time: 45 Minutes

Ingredients:

- 1 pound thick-cut bacon
- 16 ounces bowtie pasta, cooked according to package directions and drained
- 2 tomatoes, chopped
- ½ cup chopped scallions
- ½ cup Italian dressing
- ½ cup ranch dressing
- 1 tablespoon chopped fresh basil
- 1 teaspoon salt
- 1 teaspoon freshly ground black pepper
- 1 teaspoon garlic powder
- 1 head lettuce, cored and torn

Directions:

1. Supply your smoker with wood pellets and follow the start-up procedure. Preheat, with the lid closed, to 225°F.

2. Arrange the bacon slices on the grill grate, close the lid, and cook for 30 to 45 minutes, flipping after 20 minutes, until crisp.

3. Remove the bacon from the grill and chop.

4. In a large bowl, combine the chopped bacon with the cooked pasta, tomatoes, scallions, Italian dressing, ranch dressing, basil, salt, pepper, and garlic powder. Refrigerate until ready to serve.

5. Toss in the lettuce just before serving to keep it from wilting.

Mashed Red Potatoes

Servings: 4

Cooking Time: 40 Minutes

Ingredients:

- 8 Large red potatoes
- salt
- black pepper
- 1/2 Cup heavy cream
- 1/4 Cup butter

Directions:

1. Supply your smoker with wood pellets and follow the start-up procedure. Preheat the grill, with the lid closed, to 180° F.

2. Slice red potatoes in half, lengthwise then cut in half again to make quarters. Season potatoes with salt and pepper.

3. Increase the heat to High and preheat. Once the grill is hot, set potatoes directly on the grill grate. Grill: 450 °F

4. Every 15 minutes flip potatoes to ensure all sides get color. Continue to do this until potatoes are fork tender.

5. When tender, mash potatoes with cream, butter, salt, and pepper to taste. Serve warm, enjoy!

Skillet Potato Cake

Servings: 4
Cooking Time: 40 Minutes

Ingredients:

- 8 Tablespoon butter, melted
- 2 Pound russet potatoes, peeled and thinly sliced
- 3 Tablespoon kosher salt
- 2 Tablespoon freshly ground black pepper
- thyme

Directions:

1. Supply your smoker with wood pellets and follow the start-up procedure. Preheat the grill, with the lid closed, to 375° F.
2. Brush the bottom of a cast iron skillet with part of the melted butter. Place potato slices vertically around the outer edges then fill in the middle in the same fashion.
3. Pour additional melted butter over the top of the layers and sprinkle with salt and pepper.
4. Place skillet in grill and cook for 35 to 40 minutes or until potatoes are fork tender and golden brown.
5. Garnish with a sprinkle of fresh thyme over the top of the potatoes. Enjoy!

Baked Breakfast Mini Quiches

Servings: 8
Cooking Time: 15 Minutes

Ingredients:

- cooking spray
- 1 Tablespoon extra-virgin olive oil
- 1/2 yellow onion, diced
- 3 Cup Spinach, fresh
- 10 eggs
- 4 Ounce shredded cheddar, mozzarella or Swiss cheese
- 1/4 Cup fresh basil
- 1 Teaspoon kosher salt
- 1/2 Teaspoon black pepper

Directions:

1. Spray a 12-cup muffin tin generously with cooking spray.
2. In a small skillet over medium heat, warm the oil. Add the onion and cook, stirring frequently, until softened, about 7 minutes. Add the spinach and cook until wilted, about 1 minute longer.
3. Transfer to a cutting board to cool, then chop the mixture so the spinach if broken up a little.
4. Supply your smoker with wood pellets and follow the start-up procedure. Preheat the grill, with the lid closed, to 350° F.
5. In a large bowl, whisk the eggs until frothy. Add the cooled onions and spinach, cheese, basil, 1 tsp salt and 1/2 tsp pepper. Stir to combine. Divide egg mixture evenly among the muffin cups.
6. Place tray on the grill and bake until the eggs have puffed up, are set, and are beginning to brown, about 18 to 20 minutes. Grill: 350 ˚F
7. Serve immediately, or allow to cool on a wire rack, then refrigerate in an air tight container for up to 4 days. Enjoy!

Smoked Bbq Onion Brussels Sprout

Servings: 4
Cooking Time: 110 Minutes

Ingredients:

- 4 strip bacon
- 1 onion minced
- 2 cloves garlic minced

- 1 lb brussels sprouts stems trimmed and cut in half
- 1 tbsp BBQ Spice Blend
- 1/2 cup Apple Habanero Bar-B-Que Sauce (or other BBQ sauce)

Directions:

1. Supply your smoker with wood pellets and follow the start-up procedure. Preheat the grill, with the lid closed, to High heat. Place a cast iron skillet over the highest heat spot and cook the bacon until crisp.

2. Remove the bacon from pan and drain, reserving the bacon fat in the pan.

3. Reduce the heat on your smoker to 250°F.

4. Add the onions, garlic, and brussels to the pan and toss to coat in the bacon drippings. Sprinkle the BBQ spice blend over top.

5. Cover the lid and allow to smoke for 1 to 1 1/2 hours, until the sprouts are fork tender.

6. For the last 20 minutes of smoking, toss the brussels sprouts in half of the barbecue sauce.

7. Remove the sprouts from the smoker.

8. Chop the bacon and add it and the remaining barbecue sauce to the pan of sprouts, tossing to coat.

9. Serve hot.

Green Bean Casserole

Servings: 6
Cooking Time: 25 Minutes

Ingredients:

- 1/2 Stick butter
- 1 Small onion
- 1/2 Cup sliced button mushrooms
- 4 Can green beans, drained
- 2 Can cream of mushroom soup
- 1 Teaspoon Lawry's Seasoned Salt
- pepper
- 1 Can French's Original Crispy Fried Onions
- 1 Cup grated sharp cheddar cheese

Directions:

1. Supply your smoker with wood pellets and follow the start-up procedure. Preheat the grill, with the lid closed, to 375° F.

2. Melt butter in a cast iron skillet and add onions and mushrooms, stirring occasionally until softened.

3. Add drained green beans and cream of mushroom soup and stir gently to combine.

4. Season with seasoned salt and pepper and sprinkle the top with grated cheddar cheese and fried onions.

5. Bake for 25 minutes. Serve warm, enjoy! Grill: 375 °F

Braised Creamed Green Beans

Servings: 4
Cooking Time: 25 Minutes

Ingredients:

- 6 Tablespoon butter
- 2 Clove garlic, pressed or minced
- 1 shallot, thinly sliced
- 1 Cup heavy cream
- 1 Pinch ground nutmeg
- salt
- 3 Pound mixed greens such as kale, chard or collards; washed, stems removed and torn into bite sized pieces

Directions:

1. Supply your smoker with wood pellets and follow the start-up procedure. Preheat the grill, with the lid closed, to 325° F.

2. In a saucepan, heat 2 tablespoons of the butter over high heat until it foams. Add the

garlic and shallot and cook over medium-low heat, stirring, until softened and golden, about 5 minutes.

3. Add the cream, bring to a simmer and cook until slightly thickened, about 10 minutes.

4. Add the nutmeg and salt to taste. Using a hand blender, purée until smooth.

5. In a cast iron pan, heat the remaining 4 tablespoons butter over high heat until it foams.

6. Add the greens and cook until tender but still bright green, about 5 minutes.

7. Sprinkle with salt and add the cream mixture. Cover and transfer to the grill.

8. Braise greens for 15-20 minutes until the cream is bubbling and greens are tender. Grill: 325 ˚F

9. Season to taste with nutmeg and salt. Serve hot. Enjoy!

Roasted Mashed Potatoes

Servings: 8
Cooking Time: 40 Minutes

Ingredients:

- 5 Pound Yukon Gold potatoes
- 1 1/2 Stick butter, softened
- 1 1/2 Cup heavy whipping cream, room temperature
- kosher salt
- white pepper

Directions:

1. Supply your smoker with wood pellets and follow the start-up procedure. Preheat the grill, with the lid closed, to 300° F.

2. Peel and cut potatoes into 1/2 inch cubes. Place the potatoes in a shallow baking dish with 1/2 cup water and cover. Bake until tender, about 40 minutes. Grill: 300 ˚F

3. In a medium saucepan, combine cream and butter. Cook over medium heat until butter is melted.

4. Remove potatoes from the grill and drain water.

5. Transfer potatoes to a bowl and mash using a potato masher. Gradually add in cream and butter mixture and mix using the masher. Be careful not to overwork or the potatoes will becomes gluey. Season with salt and pepper to taste. Enjoy!

Smoked Pickled Green Beans

Servings: 4
Cooking Time: 45 Minutes

Ingredients:

- 1 Pound Green Beans, blanched
- 1/2 Cup salt
- 1/2 Cup sugar
- 1 Tablespoon red pepper flakes
- 2 Cup white wine vinegar
- 2 Cup ice water

Directions:

1. Supply your smoker with wood pellets and follow the start-up procedure. Preheat the grill, with the lid closed, to 180° F.

2. Place the blanched green beans on a mesh grill mat and place mat directly on the grill grate. Smoke the green beans for 30-45 minutes until they've picked up the desired amount of smoke. Remove from grill and set aside until the brine is ready. Grill: 180 ˚F

3. In a medium sized saucepan, bring all remaining ingredients, except ice water, to a boil over medium high heat on the stove. Simmer for 5-10 minutes then remove from heat and steep 20 minutes more. Pour brine over ice water to cool.

4. Once brine has cooled, pour over the green beans and weigh them down with a few plates to ensure they are completely submerged. Let sit 24 hours before use. Enjoy!

Roasted New Potatoes With Compound Butter

Servings: 4
Cooking Time: 45 Minutes

Ingredients:

- 2 Pound Small Red, White or Purple Potatoes (or Combination of All Three)
- 3 Tablespoon olive oil
- salt and pepper
- 2 Stick Butter, unsalted
- 1 Tablespoon shallot, minced
- 3 Tablespoon Finely Chopped Herbs, Such As Tarragon, Parsley, Basil or Combination
- 2 Teaspoon kosher salt

Directions:

1. Supply your smoker with wood pellets and follow the start-up procedure. Preheat the grill, with the lid closed, to 400° F. Cut the potatoes in half and place in a large mixing bowl. Cover with the olive oil, a teaspoon of salt and generous grinding of pepper.

2. Place on a large baking sheet so there is space between the potatoes. Place on the grill and roast for 45 minutes to 1 hour, until crispy skinned. Toss once during cooking. Grill: 400 ˚F

3. To make the butter: Place it in a medium sized shallow mixing bowl. Use a wooden spoon or strong spatula to break it up and soften it even more. Sprinkle the shallot, herbs, and salt over the butter, then use the spoon to combine the ingredients. Taste, adding more salt or herbs if necessary. Reserve a few tablespoons of the butter to serve on the potatoes.

4. To freeze the butter for future use, place a foot long piece of plastic wrap on the counter. Spread the butter out into a 6" log across the long direction of the plastic wrap towards the bottom. Begin to roll the plastic wrap away from you to roll it into a log, twisting the sides of the plastic wrap like a candy wrapper to secure.

5. Using your hands, shape the log into an even cylinder. Once it's wrapped tightly, place in the freezer. Then when more is needed, simply slice off coins of it to serve over grilled steak, chicken, veggies, or roasted potatoes. The butter holds well in the freezer for up to one month. Enjoy!
*Cook times will vary depending on set and ambient temperatures.

Grilled Broccoli Rabe

Servings: 4
Cooking Time: 10 Minutes

Ingredients:

- 4 Tablespoon extra-virgin olive oil
- 4 Bunch broccoli rabe or broccolini
- kosher salt
- 1 lemon, halved

Directions:

1. Supply your smoker with wood pellets and follow the start-up procedure. Preheat the grill, with the lid closed, to 450° F.

2. On a platter or in a mixing bowl, drizzle the olive oil over the broccoli rabe. Use your hands to mix thoroughly, coating the vegetables evenly with the oil. Season with sea salt.

3. Place the broccoli rabe in one layer directly on the lowest grill grate. Close the lid and cook for 5 to 10 minutes. You want there to be some color

and slight char on the first side. Flip and cook for a few more minutes. Grill: 450 ˚F

4. Transfer the broccoli rabe to a serving platter and squeeze the juice of half a lemon evenly over the top.

5. Serve with more lemon wedges on the side. Enjoy!

Salt Crusted Baked Potatoes

Servings: 4
Cooking Time: 60 Minutes

Ingredients:
- 6 russet potatoes, scrubbed and dried
- 3 Tablespoon canola oil
- 1 Tablespoon kosher salt
- butter
- sour cream
- Chives, fresh
- Bacon Bits
- cheddar cheese

Directions:
1. In a large bowl, coat the potatoes in canola oil and sprinkle heavily with salt.
2. Supply your smoker with wood pellets and follow the start-up procedure. Preheat the grill, with the lid closed, to 450° F.
3. Place the potatoes directly on the grill grate and bake for 30-40 minutes, or until soft in the middle when pricked with a fork. Serve loaded with your favorite toppings. Enjoy! Grill: 450 ˚F

Roasted Red Pepper White Bean Dip

Servings: 4
Cooking Time: 40 Minutes

Ingredients:
- 4 Whole garlic
- 4 Tablespoon extra-virgin olive oil
- 2 Bell Pepper, Red
- 3 Tablespoon Dill Weed, fresh
- 3 Tablespoon chopped flat-leaf parsley
- 2 Can cannellini beans, mashed
- 4 Teaspoon lemon juice
- 1 1/2 Teaspoon salt

Directions:
1. Roasting the garlic and red peppers:
2. Supply your smoker with wood pellets and follow the start-up procedure. Preheat the grill, with the lid closed, to 400° F.
3. Peel away the outside layers of the garlic husk. Cut off the top of the garlic bulb, exposing each of the individual cloves. Drizzle olive oil over the top of the head of garlic and rub it in. Wrap the garlic in foil, completely covering it. Put the head of garlic and the two red peppers (washed and dried) on the Traeger.
4. Roast the garlic for 25-30 minutes and the peppers for about 40 minutes. Rotate the peppers a quarter-turn every 10 minutes until the exterior is blistered and blackened. Grill: 400 ˚F
5. Pull the peppers off the grill and put them in a bowl. Cover the bowl with plastic wrap and leave them for 15 minutes. The steam will loosen the skins so that they slip off like a drumstick covered in barbecue sauce.
6. Peel off the pepper skin. Cut off the stems and scrape out the seeds and they're ready to use.
7. As for the garlic, let it cool and then pull out the individual cloves as needed.
8. The dip:
9. In a blender put the roasted red peppers, 4 cloves of roasted garlic, dill, parsley, drained and rinsed beans, olive oil, lemon juice and salt.

10. Blend until the dip is smooth and creamy. You may need to scrape down the sides of the blender a couple of times. If it's having difficulty blending or looks too thick add more olive oil or lemon juice. (Add more lemon juice if it tastes like it needs more acid or brightness.) Enjoy!

Baked Sweet Potatoes

Servings: 8
Cooking Time: 60 Minutes

Ingredients:
- 1 Cup butter, softened
- 1/4 Cup pure maple syrup
- 1/2 Teaspoon ground cinnamon
- 8 Medium sweet potatoes

Directions:
1. Make the Maple-Cinnamon Butter: In a mixing bowl, combine the butter, maple syrup, and cinnamon and whip with a wooden spoon. (Alternatively, blend the ingredients using a hand-held mixer or a stand mixer.) Transfer to a small bowl, cover, and chill until serving time.
2. Supply your smoker with wood pellets and follow the start-up procedure. Preheat the grill, with the lid closed, to 375° F. Arrange the sweet potatoes on the grill grate and bake until soft, 1 to 1-1/2 hours, depending on the size of the potatoes. Make a slit in the side of each, and squeeze the ends gently to fluff.
3. Serve hot with the Maple-Cinnamon Butter. Enjoy!

Cast Iron Potatoes

Servings: 4
Cooking Time: 60 Minutes

Ingredients:
- 4 Tablespoon butter, cut into cubes
- 2 1/2 Pound potatoes, peeled and cut into 1/8 inch slices
- 1/2 Large sweet onion, thinly sliced
- salt
- black pepper
- 1 1/2 Cup grated mild cheddar or jack cheese
- 2 Cup milk
- paprika

Directions:
1. Butter the inside of a cast iron skillet and layer half the potato slices on the bottom. Top with half the onions. Season with salt and pepper.
2. Sprinkle 1 cup of the cheese over the potatoes and onions and dot with half the butter. Layer the remaining potatoes and onions on top. Dot with remaining butter.
3. Pour the milk into the skillet. Cover the skillet tightly with aluminum foil.
4. Supply your smoker with wood pellets and follow the start-up procedure. Preheat the grill, with the lid closed, to 350° F.
5. Bake for 1 hour, or until the potatoes are very tender. Grill: 350 ˚F
6. Remove the foil and top with the remaining 1/2 cup of cheese. Bake for 30 minutes more (uncovered) until the cheese is lightly browned. Dust the top with paprika and serve immediately.

Traeger Baked Potato Torte

Servings: 6
Cooking Time: 25 Minutes

Ingredients:
- 6 Yukon Gold potatoes, sliced 1/4 inch thick
- 2 Stick butter, melted
- 3 Clove garlic, crushed
- 2 Tablespoon rosemary, chopped
- 1 Cup Parmesan cheese, grated

- salt and pepper

Directions:

1. Supply your smoker with wood pellets and follow the start-up procedure. Preheat the grill, with the lid closed, to 375° F.

2. While the Traeger is heating up, peel and slice the potatoes (make sure to put them in water so they will not oxidize). Melt the butter and combine it with the crushed garlic.

3. Grease a 12" cast iron pan with butter and start to layer the torte. The layers should go as follows, potatoes, butter garlic mixture, rosemary, parmesan, continue layering to the top of the pan, about 4 to 5 layers.

4. Place the pan in the Traeger and bake for 20 to 25 minutes, or until the potatoes are fully cooked. If the top of the torte starts to darken before it is finished cooking, reduce the heat to 325°F. Serve hot and enjoy! Grill: 375 ℉

Grilled Asparagus & Honey-glazed Carrots

Servings: 4
Cooking Time: 35 Minutes

Ingredients:

- 1 Bunch asparagus, woody ends removed
- 1 Pound Carrots, peeled
- 2 Tablespoon olive oil
- sea salt
- 2 Tablespoon honey
- lemon zest

Directions:

1. Rinse all vegetables under cold water. Drizzle asparagus with olive oil and a generous sprinkling of sea salt. Generously drizzle carrots with honey and lightly sprinkle with sea salt.

2. Supply your smoker with wood pellets and follow the start-up procedure. Preheat the grill, with the lid closed, to 350° F.

3. Place carrots on the grill first and cook for 10-15 minutes, then add asparagus and cook both for another 15 to 20 minutes, or until they're done to your liking. Grill: 350 ℉

4. Top the asparagus with some fresh lemon zest. Enjoy!

Double-smoked Cheese Potatoes

Servings: 12
Cooking Time: 35 Minutes

Ingredients:

- 4 large baking potatoes (12 to 14 ounces each—preferably organic)
- 1 1/2 tablespoons bacon fat or butter, melted, or extra virgin olive oil
- Coarse salt (sea or kosher) and freshly ground black pepper
- 4 strips artisanal bacon (like Nueske's), cut crosswise into 1/4-inch slivers
- 6 tablespoons (3/4 stick) cold unsalted butter, thinly sliced
- 2 scallions, trimmed, white and green parts finely chopped (about 4 tablespoons)
- 2 cups coarsely grated smoked or regular white cheddar cheese (about 8 ounces)
- 1/2 cup sour cream
- Spanish smoked paprika (pimentón) or sweet paprika, for sprinkling

Directions:

1. Supply your smoker with wood pellets and follow the start-up procedure. Preheat the grill, with the lid closed, to 400° F.Add enough wood for 1 hour of smoking as specified by the manufacturer.

2. Scrub the potatoes on all sides with a vegetable brush. Rinse well under cold running water and blot dry with paper towels. Prick each potato several times with a fork (this keeps the spud from exploding and facilitates the smoke absorption). Brush or rub the potato on all sides with the bacon fat and season generously with salt and pepper.

3. Place the potatoes on the smoker rack. Smoke until the skins are crisp and the potatoes are tender in the center (they'll be easy to pierce with a slender metal skewer), about 1 hour.

4. Meanwhile, place the bacon in a cold skillet and fry over medium heat until browned and crisp, 3 to 4 minutes. Drain off the bacon fat (save the fat for future potatoes).

5. Transfer the potatoes to a cutting board and let cool slightly. Cut each potato in half lengthwise. Using a spoon, scrape out most of the potato flesh, leaving a 1/4-inch-thick shell. (It's easier to scoop the potatoes when warm.) Cut the potato flesh into 1/2-inch dice and place in a bowl.

6. Add the bacon, 4 tablespoons of the butter, the scallions, and cheese to the potato flesh and gently stir to mix. Stir in the sour cream and salt and pepper to taste; the mixture should be highly seasoned. Stir as little and as gently as possible so as to leave some texture to the potatoes.

7. Spoon the potato mixture back into the potato shells, mounding it in the center. Top each potato half with a thin slice of the remaining butter and sprinkle with paprika. The potatoes can be prepared up to 24 hours ahead to this stage, covered, and refrigerated.

8. Just before serving, preheat your smoker to 400 °F. Add enough wood for 30 minutes of smoking. Place the potatoes in a shallow aluminum foil pan and re-smoke them until browned and bubbling, 15 to 20 minutes.

PORK RECIPES

Big Game Day Bbq Ribs

Servings: 6

Cooking Time: 180 Minutes

Ingredients:

- 2 Rack St. Louis-style ribs
- 1/4 Cup Big Game Rub
- 1 Cup peach nectar
- 1 Cup Apricot BBQ Sauce

Directions:

1. Wash ribs and pat dry. Pull membrane off the back of ribs.

2. Supply your smoker with wood pellets and follow the start-up procedure. Preheat the grill, with the lid closed, to 275° F.

3. Apply a thin coat of rub to the back of the ribs and all sides. Let rest 5 minutes. Turn ribs over, apply a heavy coat of rub to the top and let rest or "sweat" for 15 minutes.

4. Place ribs bone side down directly on the grill grate and cook for 2 to 2-1/2 hours. Check for doneness, the internal temperature should be 160°F and the meat should be pulling away from the bones. Grill: 275 °F Probe: 160 °F

5. Remove ribs from the grill placing them meat side down on top of a piece of foil. Pour 1/2 cup peach nectar over ribs and wrap foil tightly around the ribs creating a packet. Grill: 275 °F

6. Put ribs back on the grill, bone side up and cook for another 30 to 45 minutes or until tender, but not fall-off-the-bone. Grill: 275 °F

7. Remove from the grill and sauce the front and back of the ribs. Place the ribs back on the Traeger for 15 minutes to set the sauce.

8. Remove, let rest for 15 minutes, slice and serve. Enjoy!

Fast Ribs

Servings: 5

Cooking Time: 240 Minutes

Ingredients:

- 1 Rack Baby Back Rib
- 1 Bottle Sweet Rib Rub

Directions:

1. Remove the ribs from their packaging and pat dry. Flip to back of ribs and score the membrane with a knife, then peel off the membrane.

2. Generously sprinkle the ribs with Sweet Rib Rub on both sides of the ribs and rub.

3. Supply your smoker with wood pellets and follow the start-up procedure. Preheat the grill, with the lid open, to 250° F. Once the smoker is ready, add the ribs and smoke for 4 hours, or until the ribs are tender and the meat is pulling away from the bone.

4. Serve and enjoy!

First-timer's Pulled Pork

Servings: 8

Cooking Time: 540 Minutes

Ingredients:

- 1 bone-in pork shoulder, about 5 to 7lb (2.3 to 3.2kg)
- coarse salt
- freshly ground black pepper
- 1½ cups low-carb beer or sugar-free dark-colored soda
- for the sauce

- 1½ cups apple cider vinegar
- ½ cup distilled water
- 2 tbsp ketchup
- 1½ tbsp granulated brown sugar or low-carb substitute
- 1 tsp coarse salt, plus more
- 1 tsp freshly ground black pepper
- ½ to 1 tsp crushed red pepper flakes

Directions:

1. Supply your smoker with wood pellets and follow the start-up procedure. Preheat the grill, with the lid closed, to 250° F.

2. In a medium saucepan on the stovetop over medium-high, make the vinegar sauce by bringing the ingredients to a boil. Whisk to dissolve the sugar and salt. Let the sauce cool to room temperature and then transfer to a jar with a tight-fitting lid. Set aside.

3. Season the pork shoulder on all sides with salt and pepper. Place the pork on the grate and smoke until the bone releases easily from the meat and the internal temperature reaches 200°F (93°C), about 7 to 9 hours. Wrap the pork tightly in a large piece of heavy-duty aluminum foil and let rest in an insulated cooler for up to 1 hour.

4. Carefully remove the pork from the foil and reserve the juices. Wear heatproof gloves to pull the pork into chunks. Discard the bone and any large lumps of fat. Pull the meat into shreds and transfer to a clean aluminum foil roasting pan. Moisten with some of the reserved juices. Taste, adding more salt and pepper. Serve with the vinegar sauce.

Baby Back Ribs With Mustard Slather

Servings: 4

Cooking Time: 120 Minutes

Ingredients:

- 2 racks of baby back ribs, each about 2lb (1kg)
- all-purpose barbecue rub
- low-carb barbecue sauce (optional)
- for the mustard
- ½ cup yellow or brown mustard
- 2 tbsp dill pickle juice or apple cider vinegar

Directions:

1. Supply your smoker with wood pellets and follow the start-up procedure. Preheat the grill, with the lid closed, to 325° F.

2. Remove the thick membrane on the bone side of the ribs. Don't remove the thin membrane on top of the bones because it holds them together. Trim off any odd bits of meat or excess fat. Place the ribs on a rimmed sheet pan.

3. In a small bowl, make the mustard slather by combining the mustard and pickle juice. Brush the ribs on both sides with the mixture and then season with the barbecue rub.

4. Place the ribs on the grate and smoke until the ribs are tender, about 1½ to 2 hours. (A toothpick inserted between bones should go in with little resistance. The meat will also have pulled back from the bone about ½ inch [1.25cm].) Brush the ribs with barbecue sauce (if using) during the last 10 minutes of smoking. Place the ribs meat side down on the grate for 5 minutes. Turn and grill for 5 minutes more. This sets the sauce.

5. Transfer the ribs to a cutting board. Use a sharp knife to cut the slabs in half or into individual ribs. Serve immediately with more barbecue sauce.

St. Louis–style Pork Steaks

Servings: 4

Cooking Time: 120 Minutes

Ingredients:

- 1 cup low-carb barbecue sauce
- ¼ cup low-carb beer or sugar-free dark-colored soda or sugar-free root beer
- 4 bone-in pork shoulder steaks, each about 1lb (450g) and at least 1 inch (2.5cm) thick
- for the rub
- 1 tbsp coarse salt
- 1 tbsp freshly ground black pepper
- 1 tbsp granulated light brown sugar or low-carb substitute
- 1 tbsp sweet or smoked paprika
- 1 tsp granulated garlic or garlic powder
- 1 tsp celery salt

Directions:

1. Supply your smoker with wood pellets and follow the start-up procedure. Preheat the grill, with the lid closed, to 250° F.

2. In a small bowl, combine the barbecue sauce and beer. Set aside.

3. In a small bowl, make the rub by combining the ingredients. Mix well. Season the steaks on both sides with some of the rub.

4. Place the steaks on the grate at an angle to the bars and smoke for 30 minutes. Transfer the steaks to an aluminum foil roasting pan. Pour the barbecue mixture over them. Use tongs to turn the steaks, making sure each is coated well with the sauce.

5. Tightly wrap aluminum foil over the top of the pan and place it on the grate. Braise the steaks until they're fork tender, about 1½ hours. (Protect your hands when lifting a corner of the foil because steam will escape.)

6. Remove the pan from the grill and serve the steaks immediately.

Sweet Smoked Country Ribs

Servings: 12-15

Cooking Time: 240 Minutes

Ingredients:

- 2 pounds country-style ribs
- 1 batch Sweet Brown Sugar Rub
- 2 tablespoons light brown sugar
- 1 cup Pepsi or other cola
- ¼ cup The Ultimate BBQ Sauce

Directions:

1. Supply your smoker with wood pellets and follow the start-up procedure. Preheat the grill, with the lid closed, to 180°F.

2. Sprinkle the ribs with the rub and use your hands to work the rub into the meat.

3. Place the ribs directly on the grill grate and smoke for 3 hours.

4. Remove the ribs from the grill and place them on enough aluminum foil to wrap them completely. Dust the brown sugar over the ribs.

5. Increase the grill's temperature to 300°F.

6. Fold in three sides of the foil around the ribs and add the cola. Fold in the last side, completely enclosing the ribs and liquid. Return the ribs to the grill and cook for 45 minutes.

7. Remove the ribs from the foil and place them on the grill grate. Baste all sides of the ribs with barbecue sauce. Cook for 15 minutes more to caramelize the sauce.

8. Remove the ribs from the grill and serve immediately.

Bacon Wrapped Asparagus

Servings: 4
Cooking Time: 20 Minutes

Ingredients:
- 1 Bunch asparagus
- 1 Tablespoon olive oil
- 1/2 Teaspoon garlic powder
- 1/2 Teaspoon onion powder
- salt and pepper
- 1 Pound Bacon, sliced

Directions:
1. Coat the Asparagus evenly with olive oil, then sprinkle the asparagus evenly with, garlic powder, onion powder, salt and pepper. Individually wrap each asparagus with 1 piece of thin cut bacon.
2. Supply your smoker with wood pellets and follow the start-up procedure. Preheat the grill, with the lid closed, to 450° F.
3. Place the wrapped asparagus on the grill and roast for 15-20 minutes, or until the bacon is crispy. Enjoy!

Smoked Bacon Roses

Servings: 2
Cooking Time: 60 Minutes

Ingredients:
- 1 Pack Bacon, Thick Cut
- 1 Dozen Roses, Fake

Directions:
1. Supply your smoker with wood pellets and follow the start-up procedure. Preheat the grill, with the lid open, to 225° F.
2. Roll each piece of bacon tightly, starting on the thicker side of the strip. Take a toothpick and skewer the middle of the bottom of the bacon roll to keep the bacon from unraveling. With a second toothpick, skewer the bacon roll so that the two toothpicks form an "X" at the bottom of the roll of bacon. Do this to every piece of bacon.
3. Place the bacon rolls directly on the grates of your preheated Grill and smoke for an hour, checking on them every 20 minutes.
4. While the bacon is smoking, rip the petals of the fake roses off of the steams.
5. Once the bacon is fully cooked, remove the toothpicks and pierce the bacon in the head of the steam (where the fake flowers once were). If the bacon isn't staying, you can break a toothpick in half and stick it in the tip of the steam, press firmly and try piercing the bacon again.
6. Place in a nice vase with some babies breath and gift to your Valentine.

Beer Braised Garlic Bbq Pork Butt

Servings: 6-8
Cooking Time: 300 Minutes

Ingredients:
- One 12Oz Bottle Dark Beer
- 1/2 Cup Brown Sugar
- 2 Tablespoons Granulated Garlic
- 4 Tablespoons Honey
- 1 Cup Ketchup
- 1 Tablespoon Olive Oil
- Pulled Pork Rub
- 1 Pork Butt, Boneless
- 2 Tablespoons Worcestershire Sauce
- 4 Tablespoons Yellow Mustard

Directions:
1. Generously season the pork butt with Pulled Pork Rub, making sure to rub the seasoning in on all surfaces of roast. Place the pork onto a roasting rack inside a 9x13 pan.

2. Pour about half a bottle of dark beer into the bottom of the pan and save the remaining amount of beer, you'll need this later.

3. Supply your smoker with wood pellets and follow the start-up procedure. Preheat the grill, with the lid open, to high heat. If you're using a gas or charcoal, set it up for high direct heat. Place the pan in the center of the grill and grill for 30 minutes until the pork roast is dark in color and charred in some spots.

4. Remove the pork from the grill and decrease the temperature of the grill to 325°F. Set aside and began to make the BBQ sauce.

5. In a medium sized bowl, add ketchup, brown sugar, yellow mustard, honey, Worcestershire, granulated garlic, half bottle of dark beer, and finally 1 tbsp of Pulled Pork Rub. Mix together thoroughly.

6. Take the sauce and pour it over the roast, cover with aluminum foil.

7. Cook the roast for 4 - 6 hours or until the meat is falling apart tender and the bone easily comes away from the meat and reaches an internal temperature of 200°F. Remove the pork from the grill and allow it to rest for 10-15 minutes.

8. Shred the pork with meat claws or forks, discarding any fat or gristle. Toss the shredded pork with the barbecue sauce and serve immediately.

Grilled Bbq Pork Chops

Servings: 6
Cooking Time: 12 Minutes

Ingredients:
- 6 Thick-Cut Pork Chops
- Generous amounts BBQ rub

Directions:

1. Supply your smoker with wood pellets and follow the start-up procedure. Preheat the grill, with the lid closed, to 450° F. Place seasoned pork chops on grill. Cook 6 minutes per side, or until internal temps reach 145 °F.

2. Remove from heat and let sit for 5-10 minutes before serving.

Smoked Porchetta

Servings: 6
Cooking Time: 360 Minutes

Ingredients:
- 1 Tbs Ancho Chili Powder
- 1/2 Cup Brown Sugar
- 3 Tbs Grilling Seasoning
- 1 Tbs Chopped Italian Parsley
- 1/2 Cup Maple Syrup
- 1 Tsp Dry Oregano
- 1 Tbs Chopped Oregano, Leaves
- 1/2 Pork, Belly (Skinless)
- 1 Whole Pork, Tenderloins
- 6 Slices Prosciutto, Sliced
- 1 Tbs Chopped Rosemary, Fresh
- 1 Tbs Chopped Sage, Leaves
- 1/2 Cup Sugar, Cure

Directions:

1. Sprinkle Sugar Cure on each side and rub in. (You can cure pork belly without using Sodium Nitrite (in the cure mix) but it is much safer if you use it, so I definitely recommend it).

2. In a small bowl, mix brown sugar, maple syrup, ancho chili powder and oregano, and whisk. Slather on both sides of each pork belly piece.

3. Place pork bag (if you can find a 2 gallon or larger one) or container and refrigerate Rotate and flip each 24 hours.

4. After 3 days remove pork belly and rinse each piece thoroughly.

5. If you do not rinse well the porchetta (or bacon) will be too salty due to the sugar cure.

6. Lay pork belly skin side down on a large cutting board.

7. Lightly score the meat side with diamond cuts to allow the seasoning to penetrate.

8. Lightly sprinkle with grilling seasoning, then coat well with the herb mix.

9. Lay out the prosciutto, then lay the pork tenderloin on the pork belly.

10. Lightly sprinkle tenderloin with seasoning, and wrap the pork belly tightly around it.

11. Use cooking twine to tie up tightly.

12. Season the exterior of the pork belly lightly but evenly with grilling seasoning.

13. Supply your smoker with wood pellets and follow the start-up procedure. Preheat the grill, with the lid open, to 250° F.

14. Smoke for 6 hours, or until internal temperature reaches around 175°F.

15. Remove and allow to rest for 20 minutes. Once it cools, then slice thinly and sear in a hot skillet.

16. Let it cool again for about 10 minutes before serving.

Smoked Pork Spare Ribs

Servings: 8

Cooking Time: 240 Minutes

Ingredients:

- 2 Rack (6 lb) pork spare ribs, trimmed
- 3 Tablespoon Pork & Poultry Rub
- 1 Cup apple juice, cider or beer
- 9 Ounce BBQ Sauce

Directions:

1. Supply your smoker with wood pellets and follow the start-up procedure. Preheat the grill, with the lid closed, to 250° F.

2. If your butcher hasn't done so already, remove the silver-skin on the back of the ribs and trim off any excess fat.

3. Season the ribs on all sides with Traeger Pork & Poultry rub.

4. Arrange the racks of spare ribs on the grill grate, bone-side down and cook for 3 to 4 hours. After the first hour, spray the ribs with apple juice. Continue spraying every hour after that with apple juice. Grill: 250 ˚F

5. Start checking the temp after 2 hours. The finished internal temperature should be 203°F, about 3 to 4 hours. Grill: 250 ˚F Probe: 203 ˚F

6. When the internal temperature registers 203°F, brush the ribs on all sides with Traeger BBQ sauce of your choice. Return ribs to the grill and cook for an additional 30 to 60 minutes to tighten the sauce.

7. To serve, cut each slab in half or into individual ribs and serve with additional BBQ sauce on the side. Enjoy!

Savory Pork Belly Banh Mi

Servings: 4

Cooking Time: 420 Minutes

Ingredients:

- 2 Carrots, Sliced
- 1 Tbsp Cilantro, Minced
- 1 Tbsp Honey
- 2 Kirby Cucumbers, Sliced Thin
- 1 Lime, Zest & Juice
- 2 Tbsp Pickling Spice
- 1 Tbsp Ponzu
- 2 Lbs Pork Belly

- 1 Cup Rice Wine Vinegar
- 2 Tbsp Salt
- 4 Sandwich Buns
- 1 Small Daikon Radish, Sliced Thin
- To Taste, Smoky Salt & Cracked Pepper Rub
- 2 Tbsp Soy Sauce
- 1/2 Cup Sriracha Hot Sauce
- 4 Cloves Star Anise
- 1/2 Cup Sugar
- 1 Cup Water

Directions:

1. 30 minutes before you plan to put the belly on the smoker season liberally with the Smoky Salt and Cracked Pepper rub.

2. Supply your smoker with wood pellets and follow the start-up procedure. Preheat the grill, with the lid open, to 240° F. If using a gas or charcoal grill, set it up for low, indirect heat.

3. Place the belly on the smoker with a tin pan underneath the meat to catch the drippings. Smoke for 7 hours or until you reach an internal temp of 195 degrees. Remove the pork and let rest for 30 minutes.

4. Make the homemade pickles: Place pickling spice and star anise in a small sauce pan and toast. Once fragrant add vinegar and bring to a boil, cook for 3 minutes. Add the water, sugar, and salt and return to a boil, cook for 5 minutes. Strain the liquid and immediately pour over the vegetables, making sure the vegetables are submerged. Set in the fridge once cool.

5. Make the Sriracha Lime Sauce: Combine the sriracha, lime, soy sauce, honey, cilantro and ponzu in a mixing bowl and whisk until combined.

6. Assemble the sandwiches, placing sliced pork belly and homemade pickles on a roll before topping it with the sriracha lime sauce.

Kodiak Cakes Candied Bacon Crumble Brownies

Servings: 6
Cooking Time: 45 Minutes

Ingredients:
- 1 Box Big Bear Brownie Mix, Kodiak Cakes
- 2 eggs
- 1 Stick butter, melted
- 2 Tablespoon coconut oil
- 2 Tablespoon water
- 2 Cup cooked bacon
- 1/2 Cup Almonds, chopped
- 1/2 Cup sugar

Directions:

1. Supply your smoker with wood pellets and follow the start-up procedure. Preheat the grill, with the lid closed, to 300° F.

2. Spray an 8" baking pan with non-stick spray.

3. Empty Kodiak Cake brownie mix into a medium-size mixing bowl. Add eggs, melted butter, coconut oil, and water. Gently mix, being careful not to overmix. Pour into prepared pan.

4. Place brownies in center of grill grate; bake for 45 minutes. Grill: 300 °F

5. While the brownies are baking, begin assembling bacon crumble. Add honey or sugar to a medium-size saucepan, over high heat. Add bacon and almonds. Stir for 2-3 minutes, or until sugar has dissolved. Remove from heat and let cool.

6. Remove brownies from grill and cool completely. Sprinkle candied bacon crumble over the top of brownies. Enjoy!

Smoked Stuffed Avocado Recipe

Servings: 8

Cooking Time: 30 Minutes

Ingredients:

- 6 Whole avocados
- 3 Cup leftover pulled pork
- 1 1/2 Cup Monterey Jack cheese, shredded
- 1 Cup Salsa, tomato
- 1/4 Cup cilantro, finely chopped
- 8 Whole Quail Eggs

Directions:

1. Supply your smoker with wood pellets and follow the start-up procedure. Preheat the grill, with the lid closed, to 375° F.

2. Remove the pits from the avocados, removing some avocado from the center if needed.

3. In a bowl, mix together pork, cheese, salsa and cilantro. Place pork mixture on top of avocados and place in grill. Cook for 25 minutes.

4. Take a spoon and make a divot or "nest" for the quail egg. Carefully crack the quail egg into the "nest" and cook for an additional 5 to 8 minutes or until the egg reaches desired doneness.

5. Remove from the grill and serve. Enjoy!

Pulled Pork Stew

Servings: 4

Cooking Time: 120 Minutes

Ingredients:

- 16 Ounce salsa verde
- 15 Ounce black beans, drained and rinsed
- 15 Ounce fire roasted red peppers, drained and rinsed
- 1 Pound pulled pork
- 1 Teaspoon ground cumin
- 2 Cup chicken stock

- salt and pepper
- Avocado, Sliced

Directions:

1. Supply your smoker with wood pellets and follow the start-up procedure. Preheat the grill, with the lid closed, to 375° F.

2. Stir in salsa verde, black beans, fire-roasted tomatoes, shredded pork, cumin and chicken broth. Season with salt and pepper to taste.

3. Cook on Traeger for 1 hour stirring every 20 minutes. After 1 hour, cover Dutch oven with lid and cook an additional hour.

4. Top stew with fresh herbs, avocado and sour cream. Serve hot, enjoy!

Bbq Pork Shoulder Steaks

Servings: 4

Cooking Time: 120 Minutes

Ingredients:

- 4 (1 to 1-1/4 inch thick) pork shoulder steaks
- 1/2 Cup mustard
- Pork & Poultry Rub
- 1/2 Cup apple juice
- 1 Cup 'Que BBQ Sauce

Directions:

1. Slather the pork steaks on all sides with the mustard and season with the Traeger Pork & Poultry Rub. (The mustard will help keep the pork moist, but the taste will be unnoticeable in the final product.)

2. Supply your smoker with wood pellets and follow the start-up procedure. Preheat the grill, with the lid closed, to 180° F.

3. Arrange the steaks on the grill grate. Smoke for 1-1/2 hours. Grill: 180 °F

4. Remove the pork steaks to a plate and increase temperature to 225°F. Preheat 5 to 10 minutes. Grill: 225 °F

5. Meanwhile, wrap each steak with aluminum foil, adding in a couple tablespoons of apple juice.

6. Cook the steaks for another hour or so or until they are tender (about 160°F on an instant-read meat thermometer). Grill: 225 °F Probe: 160 °F

7. The last 15 minutes, take the pork steaks out of the foil and put them directly on the grill.

8. Brush each steak on both sides with the Traeger 'Que BBQ Sauce or your favorite barbecue sauce.

9. Let the steaks rest for 3 minutes before serving. Enjoy!

Baked Honey Glazed Ham

Servings: 8
Cooking Time: 120 Minutes

Ingredients:
- 1 (6-8 lb) Snake River Farms Kurobuta Half Bone-In Ham
- 20 whole cloves
- 1 Stick butter, softened
- 1/4 Cup dark corn syrup
- 1 Cup honey, room temperature

Directions:
1. Supply your smoker with wood pellets and follow the start-up procedure. Preheat the grill, with the lid closed, to 325° F.

2. Score ham. Smear the entire ham with softened butter and stud with the whole cloves and place ham in foil-lined pan.

3. Combine the dark corn syrup and honey. Warm to combine if needed. Pour 3/4 of the glaze over ham, and bake for 1-1/2 to 2 hours on the grill or until the ham reaches 140°F. Grill: 325 °F Probe: 140 °F

4. Baste ham every 20 minutes with remaining honey glaze. Grill: 325 °F Probe: 140 °F

5. Remove from grill and let rest a few minutes.

6. Slice and serve. Enjoy!

St. Louis Bbq Ribs

Servings: 4
Cooking Time: 240 Minutes

Ingredients:
- 2 Rack St. Louis-style ribs
- 1/4 Cup Pork & Poultry Rub
- 1 Cup apple juice
- 1 Bottle Sweet & Heat BBQ Sauce

Directions:
1. Trim ribs and peel off membrane from the back of ribs. Apply an even coat of rub to the front and back of ribs. Let sit for 20 minutes and up to 4 hours if refrigerated.

2. Supply your smoker with wood pellets and follow the start-up procedure. Preheat the grill, with the lid closed, to 225° F.

3. Place ribs bone side down on grill grate. Put apple juice in a spray bottle and evenly spray ribs. Grill: 225 °F

4. After 3 hours, remove ribs from grill and wrap them in aluminum foil. Leave an opening at one end, pour in remainder of apple juice (about 6 oz) into the foil and wrap tightly.

5. Place ribs back on grill, meat side down and smoke for an additional 3 hours. Grill: 225 °F Probe: 203 °F

6. After 1 hour, start checking the internal temperature of ribs. Ribs are done when the internal temperature reaches 203°F. Grill: 225 °F

7. When ribs are done, remove from the foil and brush a light layer of sauce on the front and back on the ribs.

8. Return to the grill and cook an additional 10 minutes to set the sauce. Grill: 225 ˚F

9. After sauce has set, take ribs off the grill and let rest for 10 minutes. To serve, slice ribs in between the bones. Enjoy!

Barbecued Tenderloin

Servings: 4-6
Cooking Time: 30 Minutes

Ingredients:
- 2 (1-pound) pork tenderloins
- 1 batch Sweet and Spicy Cinnamon Rub

Directions:
1. Supply your smoker with wood pellets and follow the start-up procedure. Preheat the grill, with the lid closed, to 350°F.

2. Generously season the tenderloins with the rub. Using your hands, work the rub into the meat.

3. Place the tenderloins directly on the grill grate and smoke until their internal temperature reaches 145°F.

4. Remove the tenderloins from the grill and let them rest for 5 to 10 minutes, before thinly slicing and serving.

Maple Baked Ham

Servings: 8
Cooking Time: 60 Minutes

Ingredients:
- 1 (14-16 lb) ham
- whole cloves
- 1/2 Cup pure maple syrup
- 1/2 Cup brown sugar
- 1/2 Cup apple juice
- 1 Tablespoon brown mustard
- ground cinnamon
- ground ginger

Directions:
1. Supply your smoker with wood pellets and follow the start-up procedure. Preheat the grill, with the lid closed, to 325° F.

2. Score the ham all over in a diamond pattern, cutting to a depth of about 3/4 inch. Insert a clove into each intersection or "X" of the diamond pattern.

3. In a saucepan, stir together the maple syrup, brown sugar, apple juice, brown mustard, cinnamon and ginger and simmer over medium heat until brown sugar has melted. Set aside and keep warm.

4. Place ham in large roasting pan lined with aluminum foil. Place pan on grill and cook for 1-1/2 hours. Grill: 325 ˚F

5. Open grill and glaze ham with reserved mixture. Continue cooking for another 30 minutes or until a thermometer inserted into the thickest part of the meat reaches an internal temperatures of 135˚F. Grill: 325 ˚F Probe: 135 ˚F

6. Remove ham from grill and allow to rest covered with foil for 20 minutes before serving. Warm remaining sauce and serve with ham if desired. Enjoy!

Bacon-draped Injected Pork Loin Roast

Servings: 4
Cooking Time: 180 Minutes

Ingredients:
- 1 Cup apple juice

- 1/4 Cup water
- 1 Teaspoon salt
- 1 Teaspoon Worcestershire sauce
- 3 Pound (3 lb) center-cut pork loin
- Sweet Rub
- 10 Slices bacon

Directions:

1. In a small bowl combine apple juice, water, salt, and Worcestershire; stir to dissolve the salt crystals.Plunge the injector into the sauce and retract the needle to draw up the liquid. Liberally inject the meat.

2. Plunge the injector into the sauce and retract the needle to draw up the liquid. Liberally inject the meat.

3. Season the meat all over with the Traeger Sweet Rub.

4. Supply your smoker with wood pellets and follow the start-up procedure. Preheat the grill, with the lid closed, to 225° F.

5. Drape the loin with the bacon slices. Put the roast directly on the grill grate and smoke for 3 to 4 hours, or until the internal temperature of the meat is at least 145 degrees F on an instant-read thermometer. Grill: 225 ˚F Probe: 145 ˚F

6. Transfer the pork to a cutting board and let rest for 10 minutes before carving and serving. Enjoy!

Baked Maple And Brown Sugar Bacon

Servings: 4
Cooking Time: 60 Minutes

Ingredients:
- 1 Pound cold bacon
- 1/2 Cup pure maple syrup, warmed
- 1/2 Cup brown sugar, plus more as needed

Directions:

1. Supply your smoker with wood pellets and follow the start-up procedure. Preheat the grill, with the lid closed, to 300° F.

2. Line a rimmed baking sheet with foil and place a wire rack on top. Lay bacon strips in a single layer on the wire rack.

3. Using a pastry brush, brush each strip of bacon on both sides with the warmed maple syrup, then sprinkle brown sugar evenly on both sides.

4. Put the baking sheet in the grill and cook bacon for 60-75 minutes, or until bacon browns and appears to be crisping. Grill: 300 ˚F

5. Allow the bacon to cool slightly before eating. Enjoy!

Spiced Orange Ribs

Servings: 4
Cooking Time: 180 Minutes

Ingredients:
- 1 Tablespoon Adobo Sauce
- 2 (2 1⁄2-Pound) Racks Baby Back Rib
- 1⁄3 Cup Firmly Packed Light Brown Sugar
- 1 Tablespoon Chili Powder
- 5 In Adobo Sauce Chipotle Peppers
- 1⁄3 Cup Leaves Cilantro, Fresh
- 1 Teaspoon Ground Cumin
- 1⁄4 Cup Honey
- 1⁄4 Cup Ketchup
- 2 Tablespoons Lime Juice
- 1 Cup Orange Juice, Fresh
- 5 Tablespoons Sweet Heat Rub

Directions:

1. First, make the barbecue sauce. Into the bowl of a blender, add ¾ cup of orange juice, cilantro, honey, ketchup, lime juice, 2 chipotles in adobo, adobo sauce, and 1 tablespoon of the Sweet Heat

Rub. Place the lid on the blender and blend until completely smooth. Pour into a bowl, reserve ½ cup and set aside.

2. Prepare the ribs. Using the paper towels, pull the membrane off of the back of the ribs and discard. In the bowl of a blender, add the orange juice, brown sugar, chipotle peppers, chili powder, ground cumin, and Sweet Heat. Place the lid on the blender and blend until smooth. Pour this mixture over the ribs and massage into the meat. Place the ribs in the refrigerator and marinade for 8 hours.

3. Supply your smoker with wood pellets and follow the start-up procedure. Preheat the grill, with the lid open, to 275° F. Place the ribs, meat side up, and grill for 1 ½ hours. Baste the ribs with the reserved barbecue sauce, then BBQ for another 1 ½ hours, or until the ribs are extremely tender. Remove the ribs from the grill and serve with barbecue sauce.

Baked Beans

Servings: 12

Cooking Time: 180 Minutes

Ingredients:
- 1 Pack Bacon
- 1/2 Cup Brown Sugar
- 1 Coca Cola, Can
- 2 Cans Mixed Beans
- 1/3 Cup Molasses
- 4 Cans Pork And Beans
- 1 Red Onion, Chopped
- 1/3 Cup Yellow Mustard

Directions:

1. Supply your smoker with wood pellets and follow the start-up procedure. Preheat the grill, with the lid closed, to 275° F.

2. Combine all the ingredients and stir until combined.

3. Smoked for 2.5 hours covered. For the last 30 minutes, smoke uncovered.

4. Serve hot. Enjoy!

Apple-smoked Bacon

Servings: 4-6

Cooking Time: 30 Minutes

Ingredients:
- 1 (1-pound) package thick-sliced bacon

Directions:

1. Supply your smoker with wood pellets and follow the start-up procedure. Preheat the grill, with the lid closed, to 275°F.

2. Supply your smoker with wood pellets and follow the start-up procedure. Preheat the grill, with the lid closed, to 275°F.

POULTRY RECIPES

Delicious Sweet And Sour Chicken Drumsticks

Servings: 4
Cooking Time: 150 Minutes

Ingredients:
- 3 Tbsp Brown Sugar
- 8 Chicken Drumsticks
- Garlic, Minced
- Ginger, Minced
- 2 Tbsp Honey
- 1 Cup Ketchup
- ½ Lemon Lemon, Juice
- 1/2 Lime, Juiced
- 2 Tbsp Rice Wine Vinegar
- ¼ Cup Soy Sauce
- 1 Tbsp Sweet Heat Rub

Directions:
1. In a mixing bowl, combine the ketchup, soy sauce, rice wine vinegar, brown sugar, honey, ginger, garlic, lemon, lime and Sweet Heat Rub. Reserve half of the mixture for dipping sauce and set aside. Use the remaining half and pour into a large resealable plastic bag. Add the drumsticks and seal bag. Refrigerate for at least 4-12 hours. Remove chicken from bag, discarding marinade.

2. Supply your smoker with wood pellets and follow the start-up procedure. Preheat the grill, with the lid open, to 225° F. If you're using a gas or charcoal grill, set it up for low-medium heat. Smoke the chicken over indirect heat with grill lid closed for 2 – 3 hours, turning once or twice, until the chicken reaches 180°F. During the last half hour, feel free to brush more glaze on.

3. Remove from grill, and let stand for 10 minutes. Feel free to add more sauce if desired or use it as a dipping sauce for the drumsticks.

Smoked Buffalo Fries

Servings: 4
Cooking Time: 30 Minutes

Ingredients:
- 4 Chicken Breast
- salt
- black pepper
- 2 Cup Blue Cheese Dressing
- 1/2 Cup Frank's RedHot Sauce
- 1 Celery, stalks
- 6 russet potatoes
- Oil, For Frying

Directions:
1. Supply your smoker with wood pellets and follow the start-up procedure. Preheat the grill, with the lid closed, to 325° F.

2. Season chicken breast with salt and pepper. Smoke for 25-30 minutes or until 165 degrees. Pull and set aside.

3. Whisk blue cheese dressing and hot sauce together in a bowl; set aside.

4. Soak cut celery (2" long sticks) in cold water until serving

5. Cut potatoes into ¼ in sticks, resembling French fries.

6. Heat oil to 375 degrees in a Dutch oven or deep pot and gently place in potatoes. Fry until golden brown, drain on a sheet pan lined with paper towels. Season with kosher or sea salt. Repeat until all the potatoes are cooked. Keep them warm in an oven until you are ready to serve.

7. To assemble, place fries on a platter or wood board lined with butchers paper. Drizzle with franks sauce mixture, then the pulled chicken. Garnish with celery and serve immediately. Enjoy!

Chicken Corn Fritters

Servings: 8

Cooking Time: 45 Minutes

Ingredients:
- 2 Tsp Baking Powder
- 1 Cup Cheddar Jack Cheese, Shredded
- 1 1/2 Lbs Chicken Breast, Bone-In
- 3/4 Cup Corn Kernels, Drained
- 2 Eggs
- 3/4 Cup Flour
- 1 1/2 Tsp Lemon Juice
- 3 Tbsp Mayonnaise
- Olive Oil
- 2 Tbsp Parsley, Chopped
- 2 Tsp Champion Chicken Seasoning, Divided
- 1 Tbsp Scallions, Chopped
- 2 Tbsp Sour Cream
- 1 Yellow Onion, Chopped
- 1/3 Cup Milk

Directions:
1. Supply your smoker with wood pellets and follow the start-up procedure. Preheat the grill, with the lid open, to 425° F. If using a gas or charcoal grill, set it up for medium-high heat.
2. Remove skin from chicken breast. Drizzle chicken with olive oil, then season with 1 teaspoon of Champion Chicken. Place directly on grill grate, over indirect heat and grill for 25 minutes, until internal temperature is 165° F. Remove from the grill and rest for 10 minutes, then pull chicken.

3. In a mixing bowl combine onion, corn, eggs, parsley, milk, cheese, and pulled chicken.
4. In a separate mixing bowl, whisk together remaining teaspoon of Champion Chicken, flour and baking powder. Combine with the wet ingredients, then cover with plastic wrap and refrigerate for 2 hours.
5. Prepare dip: whisk together mayonnaise, sour cream, scallions, parsley, and lemon juice. Refrigerate until fritters are ready to serve.
6. Preheat griddle over medium-low flame.
7. Drizzle vegetable oil on the griddle, then add ¼ cup of fritter mixture to the griddle and cook 3 to 4 minutes per side, adding additional oil if needed.
8. Transfer fritters to a wire rack lined sheet tray. Allow to cool for 2 minutes, then serve warm with dip.

Roasted Tingle Wings

Servings: 6

Cooking Time: 30 Minutes

Ingredients:
- 3 Whole jalapeño
- 1 Tablespoon Trappey's Red Devil Cayenne Pepper Sauce
- 1/2 Cup Texas Spicy BBQ Sauce
- 2 Tablespoon Blackened Saskatchewan Rub
- 1/2 Cup honey
- 1 Tablespoon Worcestershire sauce
- 1/4 Cup water

Directions:
1. For the sauce, place all ingredients except the wings into a blender and mix until smooth.
2. Pour the sauce into a resealable plastic bag and place the wings in the bag, turning to coat thoroughly. Marinate for 1 hour to overnight.

3. Supply your smoker with wood pellets and follow the start-up procedure. Preheat the grill, with the lid closed, to 350° F.

4. Place wings directly on the gill grate and cook for 30 minutes or until wings reach an internal temperature of 165 degrees F. Enjoy!

Cranberry Turkey Breast

Servings: 6
Cooking Time: 90 Minutes

Ingredients:
- 1 Bay Leaf
- 1/2 Tsp Black Pepper
- 3 Tbsp Butter, Divided
- 1 Celery Rib, Chopped
- To Taste, Cracked Black Pepper
- 4 Oz Cremini Mushrooms
- 1/2 Cup Dried Cranberries
- 2 Garlic Cloves, Minced
- 1 Package, Approx 2Lbs Honeysuckle White Turkey Breast, Boneless
- 1/2 Cup Marsala Wine
- 1 Tbsp Olive Oil
- 1 Rosemary Sprigs
- 1/2 Tsp Rubbed Sage
- 1/2 Tsp Salt
- To Taste, Sea Salt
- 6 Oz Stuffing Mix
- 1 1/4 Cup Turkey Stock, Divided
- 1 Yellow Onion, Chopped

Directions:

1. Supply your smoker with wood pellets and follow the start-up procedure. Preheat the grill, with the lid closed, to 325° F. If using a gas or charcoal grill, set it up for medium-low heat.

2. Melt the butter 1 tablespoon of butter and olive oil in a large skillet over medium heat. Add the onions and celery and cook, stirring frequently, until soft, 3 minutes.

3. Add the garlic and mushrooms and continue to cook for 5 minutes, until the mushrooms are slightly browned.

4. Deglaze with marsala wine, using a wooden spoon to scrape up any browned bits from the bottom of the pan.

5. Add the dried cranberries, black pepper, sage, and salt and simmer for 2 minutes, then remove from the heat.

6. Fold the stuffing into the vegetable mixture, then slowly pour over turkey stock, until stuffing is moistened.

7. Place the Honeysuckle White® Turkey Breast on a large cutting board, skin-side down, then butterfly it. Season with salt and pepper, then spoon over ⅓ of the stuffing, leaving an inch border.

8. Roll the turkey breast, starting at the side with less skin. Use butcher's twine to truss the turkey breast and secure the stuffing. Place in a cast iron skillet, top remaining butter, season with salt and pepper. Place a sprig of rosemary on top, add remaining ¼ cup of stock around the turkey, along with 1 bay leaf. Transfer to the grill.

9. Cook the turkey for 1 to 1 ½ hours, until an internal temperature of 165°F is reached.

10. Remove stuffed turkey breast from the grill, rest for 15 minutes, then slice and serve warm, with remaining stuffing.

Skinny Smoked Chicken Breasts

Servings: 4-6
Cooking Time: 85 Minutes

Ingredients:
- 2½ pounds boneless, skinless chicken breasts

- Salt
- Freshly ground black pepper

Directions:

1. Supply your smoker with wood pellets and follow the start-up procedure. Preheat the grill, with the lid closed, to 180°F.

2. Season the chicken breasts all over with salt and pepper.

3. Place the breasts directly on the grill grate and smoke for 1 hour.

4. Increase the grill's temperature to 325°F and continue to cook until the chicken's internal temperature reaches 170°F. Remove the breasts from the grill and serve immediately.

Smoked Beer Brine Hens

Servings: 4
Cooking Time: 150 Minutes

Ingredients:

- 2 Tbsp Ales Pepper
- 12 Cups Beer Brine
- 2 Cornish Game Hens
- 2 Lemons
- 6 Rosemary Sprigs
- Salt & Freshly Ground Black Pepper
- 12 Thyme Sprigs

Directions:

1. Supply your smoker with wood pellets and follow the start-up procedure. Preheat the grill, with the lid open, to 300° F. (I have found the setting the grill at 300 will keep the top smoker temp between 200°F and 215°F, this could vary depending on the air temp and general weather conditions. You want to keep the upper smoking cabinet between 200°F and 215°F) If you're using a vertical smoker, set temp to 200°F.

2. Stuff your hens with the rosemary, thyme, and lemons. Coat the skin with the ales pepper and freshly ground black pepper.

3. Truss your hens and tie a small loop at the legs so you can hang your birds. Hang them in the smoker and insert a probe thermometer, cook to an internal temp of 155°F.

4. Remove the hens to rest. Final temp should be 160°F.

5. Serve these with some great creamed kale or charred asparagus.

Smoked Apple Chicken Leg Quarters

Servings: 8
Cooking Time: 120 Minutes

Ingredients:

- 8 leg quarters
- 1 bottle marinade
- Pork & chicken rub
- 1 cup of apple juice or water

Directions:

1. Rinse chicken and pat dry.

2. Marinade chicken in the fridge for at least 30 minutes or overnight (preferred).

3. Once the chicken is marinated, sprinkle both sides with the rub.

4. Supply your smoker with wood pellets and follow the start-up procedure. Preheat the grill, with the lid closed, to 225° F.

5. Place a small stainless steel pot of apple juice or water in the inside corner to help keep moist.

6. Place chicken on your grill, skin side up, with lid closed.

7. Smoke for 2 hours or until the internal temperature in the thickest part of a thigh is 165 °F.

8. Remove chicken from the grill and let it rest for 5 minutes before serving. Enjoy!

Smoked Deviled Eggs

Servings: 4
Cooking Time: 30 Minutes

Ingredients:

- 7 hard boiled eggs, cooked and peeled
- 3 Tablespoon mayonnaise
- 3 Teaspoon diced chives
- 1 Teaspoon brown mustard
- 1 Teaspoon apple cider vinegar
- hot sauce
- salt and pepper
- 2 Tablespoon cooked bacon, crumbled
- paprika

Directions:

1. Supply your smoker with wood pellets and follow the start-up procedure. Preheat the grill, with the lid closed, to 180° F.

2. Place cooked and peeled eggs directly on the grill grate and smoke eggs for 30 minutes. Grill: 180 ℉

3. Remove from grill and allow eggs to cool. Slice the eggs lengthwise and scoop the egg yolks into a gallon zip top bag.

4. Add mayonnaise, chives, mustard, vinegar, hot sauce, salt, and pepper to the bag. Zip the bag closed and, using your hands, knead all of the ingredients together until completely smooth.

5. Squeeze the yolk mixture into one corner of the bag and cut a small part of the corner off. Pipe the yolk mixture into the hard boiled egg whites. Top the deviled eggs with crumbled bacon and paprika. Chill until ready to serve. Enjoy!

Smoked Chicken Fajita Quesadillas

Servings: 4
Cooking Time: 45 Minutes

Ingredients:

- 2 Chicken, Boneless/Skinless
- 1 Tsp Chilli, Powder
- 1 Tsp Garlic Powder
- 1/2 Green Bell Pepper, Sliced
- 1 Cup Mexican Cheese, Shredded
- 1/2 Onion, Sliced
- 1/2 Tsp Oregano
- 1 Tsp Paprika, Powder
- 1/4 Tsp Pepper
- 1/2 Red Bell Peppers
- Salsa
- Sour Cream
- 4 Tortilla
- 1/2 Yellow Bell Pepper, Sliced

Directions:

1. Supply your smoker with wood pellets and follow the start-up procedure. Preheat the grill, with the lid open, to 350° F.

2. Combine spices in a bowl and season chicken breasts. Leave a little bit of seasoning for the vegetables.

3. Place chicken on the grates and cook for 30 minutes, flipped halfway through.

4. In a Vegetable Basket, combine all vegetables and season with the remaining spice mixture.

5. Open up the flame broiler and saute over the open flame for about 15 minutes, or until the vegetables are cooked to your liking.

6. On a tortilla, layer cheese, vegetables, sliced chicken and more cheese. Fold the tortilla and place over the open flame on your Grill. Sear until the tortilla is nicely toasted and the cheese is melted. Cut and serve with salsa and sour cream.

Smoked Chicken Legs

Servings: 6

Cooking Time: 110 Minutes

Ingredients:

- 1/4 Cup Brown Sugar
- 1/2 Tsp Or To Taste Cayenne Pepper
- 6 Chicken, Drumsticks
- 1 Cup Of Your Favorite Cola
- 2 Tbs Competition Chicken Seasoning
- 1 Tbs Honey
- 1/2 Tsp To Taste Hot Sauce
- 1 Cup Ketchup
- 2 Tbs   Hot Wing Sauce

Directions:

1. For the chicken: Supply your smoker with wood pellets and follow the start-up procedure. Preheat the grill, with the lid closed, to 300° F.

2. In a small bowl,Pour hot sauce over legs and toss to coat.

3. Sprinkle legs with Competition Chicken Seasoning and Hot Wing Seasoning.

4. Toss to evenly distribute seasoning.

5. Place legs in Grills Wing Rack or lay on grill.

6. Cook for 1 hour 45 minutes, or until legs reach an internal temperature of 170 degrees.

7. Brush legs with sauce and return to grill for 5-10 minutes to allow sauce to cook onto meat.

8. Serve with extra sauce on the side.Place all ingredients into a small sauce pan and whisk.

9. Bring to a boil then immediately reduce to a simmer, whisking often

10. Allow to simmer for 15 minutes or until sauce is beginning to thicken

11. Remove from heat and allow to cool

12. Pork or Beef, chicken does not have as much intramuscular fats that need to render out to result in tender meat

13. You can cook chicken at a hotter temperature to ensure you get tender, moist chicken every time

14. Use a meat thermometer to know exactly when to pull the chicken off the grill

15. I pull white meat at 165 degrees, and dark meat, such as these legs, at 175 degrees

Asian Bbq Chicken

Servings: 4

Cooking Time: 60 Minutes

Ingredients:

- 1 Whole whole chicken
- Asian BBQ Rub
- 1 Whole ginger ale

Directions:

1. Rinse chicken in cold water and pat dry with paper towels. Cover the chicken all over with Traeger Asian BBQ rub; make sure to drop some in the inside too. Place in large bag or bowl and cover and refrigerate for 12 to 24 hours.

2. Supply your smoker with wood pellets and follow the start-up procedure. Preheat the grill, with the lid closed, to 375° F.

3. Open your can of ginger ale and take a few big gulps. Set the can of soda on a stable surface. Take the chicken out of the fridge and place the bird over top of the soda can. The base of the can and the two legs of the chicken should form a sort of tripod to hold the chicken upright.

4. Stand the chicken in the center of your hot grate and cook the chicken till the skin is golden brown and the internal temperature is about 165°F on a instant-read thermometer, approximately 40 minutes to 1 hour.

5. De-throne chicken. Enjoy!

Smoked Boneless Chicken Thighs

Servings: 8 - 10
Cooking Time: 55 Minutes

Ingredients:

- 2 Tbsp Ginger Root, Grated
- 5 Lbs. Boneless Skinless Chicken Thighs
- ⅔ Cup Brown Sugar
- 2 Cups Chicken Broth
- 1 Tsp Chinese Five-Spice Powder
- 5 Garlic Cloves, Minced
- ¼ Cup Honey
- 1 Tbsp Sweet Heat Rub
- ½ Cup Soy Sauce
- 1 Yellow Onion, Minced

Directions:

1. Supply your smoker with wood pellets and follow the start-up procedure. Preheat the grill, with the lid closed, to 225° F. If using a gas or charcoal grill, set it up for low heat.
2. Remove chicken from marinade and place on a metal sheet tray. Using a mesh strainer, strain the marinade directly into a cast iron skillet.
3. Place skillet with marinade and chicken on the grill. Allow chicken to smoke for 10 minutes, then increase grill temperature to 400°F.
4. Grill an additional 15 minutes. Make sure to stir marinade periodically. The sauce will begin to reduce and thicken as it cooks.
5. After 15 minutes, baste chicken thighs with marinade, then flip and baste the other sides. Grill an additional 15 minutes, then baste again.
6. Cook until glaze has caramelized and thickened, then remove from grill and serve hot.

Bourbon Chicken Waffles

Servings: 8
Cooking Time: 30 Minutes

Ingredients:

- 1 Shot Of Bourbon
- 3 Cups Bread Crumbs
- 4 Horizontally Half Sliced Boneless, Skinless Chicken Breast
- Butter Flavored Cooking Spray
- 3 Eggs
- 1 Tsp Garlic Powder
- 1 Tsp Paprika, Powder
- Red Velvet Cake Mix
- 16 Oz. Reduced Fat Sour Cream
- Sweet Rib Rub
- ¼ Cup Vegetable Oil
- 1 ¼ Cup Water
- 1 Tbsp Worcestershire Sauce

Directions:

1. Supply your smoker with wood pellets and follow the start-up procedure. Preheat the grill, with the lid closed, to 350° F. If you're using a gas or charcoal grill, set up the grill for medium heat.
2. In a large bowl, combine the sour cream, bourbon, Worcestershire sauce, paprika, garlic powder, and Sweet Rib Rub seasoning. Add the chicken, turn the chicken breasts to coat, and cover the bowl. Refrigerate for 4-12 hrs.
3. Remove the chicken from the refrigerator and drain the marinade from the chicken. Mix together 3 cups bread crumbs and 2 tbsp Sweet Rib Rub. Mix the coating together and bread the chicken breasts.
4. Moisten a paper towel with cooking oil and using a pair of tongs, lightly grease the grill rack.
5. Grill or smoke until the internal temperature of the chicken reaches 170°F and the chicken is crispy and golden brown.

6. While the chicken is cooking, mix the eggs, vegetable oil, water, and red velvet cake mix in a bowl with the electric mixer.

7. Add the mix into the waffle iron and cook. Make as many waffles as the mix allows.

8. On a plate, place the cooked chicken on top of the waffles and top with maple syrup or honey.

Traeger Mandarin Wings

Servings: 2

Cooking Time: 30 Minutes

Ingredients:

- 1 Bottle (12 oz) mandarin orange sauce
- Beef Rub
- Chicken Rub
- 2 Pound chicken wings, flats and drumettes separated

Directions:

1. Coat chicken wings with mandarin sauce. Sprinkle Traeger Beef Rub and Traeger Chicken Rub onto wings. Marinate for at least 30 minutes.

2. Supply your smoker with wood pellets and follow the start-up procedure. Preheat the grill, with the lid closed, to 350° F.

3. Place wings directly on the grill grate and cook for 30 minutes. Enjoy! Grill: 350 °F Probe: 165 °F

Cornish Game Hens

Servings: 4

Cooking Time: 60 Minutes

Ingredients:

- 4 Cornish game hens
- 4 Tablespoon butter, melted
- Chicken Rub
- 4 Sprig rosemary or sage, plus more for garnish

Directions:

1. Rinse the Cornish game hens under cold running water, inside and out. (Game hens do not usually come with giblets, but check the cavity for them before rinsing. If you find giblets, freeze them for chicken stock, if desired.)

2. Dry thoroughly with paper towels. Tuck the wings behind the backs and tie the legs together with butcher's string.

3. Rub the outside of each hen with the melted butter. Season with Traeger Chicken Rub. Slip a sprig of rosemary into the main cavity of each hen.

4. Supply your smoker with wood pellets and follow the start-up procedure. Preheat the grill, with the lid closed, to 375° F.

5. Roast the hens for 50 to 60 minutes, or until the juices run clear and the internal temperature of the thigh, when read on an instant-read meat thermometer, is 165°F. Grill: 375 °F Probe: 165 °F

6. Transfer the hens to a platter or plates and let rest for 5 minutes.

7. Garnish with a sprig of rosemary before serving. Enjoy!

Duck Breast With Pomegranate Sauce

Servings: 4

Cooking Time: 13 Minutes

Ingredients:

- 4 duck breasts, each about 6oz (170g), skin on
- for the rub
- 2 tsp coarse salt
- 1 tsp ground cumin
- 1 tsp ground coriander
- 1 tsp freshly ground black pepper
- ½ tsp ground cinnamon

- ½ tsp ground fennel
- for the sauce
- 1 shallot, peeled and minced
- 1 cup pomegranate juice
- 1 tbsp sherry vinegar or balsamic vinegar
- 1 tsp cornstarch
- ¼ cup chicken stock or chicken broth
- 1 tbsp chilled unsalted butter, cut into 4 pieces
- ¼ cup fresh pomegranate seeds (optional)
- 1 tbsp minced fresh chives

Directions:

1. Place a cast iron skillet on the grate. Supply your smoker with wood pellets and follow the start-up procedure. Preheat the grill, with the lid closed, to 400° F.

2. In a small bowl, make the rub by combining the ingredients. Use a sharp knife to diagonally score the skin of each duck breast—but don't nick the flesh. Lightly season the scored side of each breast.

3. Place the duck breasts skin side down in the skillet and sear until the skin is crisp and golden brown, about 8 to 10 minutes. Turn the breasts and cook until the internal temperature in the thickest part of a breast reaches 130°F (54°C), about 2 to 3 minutes more. Transfer the breasts to a plate.

4. In a large saucepan on the stovetop over medium heat, make the sauce by heating 1 tablespoon of duck fat from the skillet. (Reserve the remainder for another use.) Add the shallot and sauté until soft, about 2 to 3 minutes.

5. Add the pomegranate juice and bring the mixture to a boil over medium-high heat. Reduce the sauce by half, about 3 to 5 minutes. Add the vinegar and lower the heat to medium low.

6. Whisk together the cornstarch and chicken stock until smooth. Whisk into the sauce and cook until the sauce thickens, about 1 to 2 minutes. Whisk in the butter and stir in the pomegranate seeds (if using).

7. Place the duck breasts on a warm platter. Drizzle the pomegranate sauce over the top. Scatter the chives around the platter before serving.

Smoked Turkey Wings

Servings: 2
Cooking Time: 60 Minutes

Ingredients:
- 4 turkey wings
- 1 batch Sweet and Spicy Cinnamon Rub

Directions:

1. Supply your smoker with wood pellets and follow the start-up procedure. Preheat the grill, with the lid closed, to 180°F.

2. Using your hands, work the rub into the turkey wings, coating them completely.

3. Place the wings directly on the grill grate and cook for 30 minutes.

4. Increase the grill's temperature to 325°F and continue to cook until the turkey's internal temperature reaches 170°F. Remove the wings from the grill and serve immediately.

Bourbon-brined Turkey Thighs

Servings: 4
Cooking Time: 135 Minutes

Ingredients:
- 4 skin-on, bone-in turkey thighs, about 2lb (1kg) total
- 6 tbsp unsalted butter, at room temperature
- 4 large fresh sage leaves

- coarse salt
- freshly ground black pepper
- for the brine
- 1 quart (1 liter) distilled water
- ¼ cup coarse salt, plus more
- ¼ cup light brown sugar or low-carb substitute
- ¼ cup bourbon (optional)

Directions:

1. In a saucepan on the stovetop over medium-high heat, make the brine by combining the water, salt, brown sugar, and bourbon (if using). Bring to a boil. Stir until the salt and sugar dissolve. Remove the saucepan from the stovetop and let the brine cool to room temperature.

2. Place the turkey in a resealable plastic bag and pour the brine over the thighs. Refrigerate for 4 hours.

3. Supply your smoker with wood pellets and follow the start-up procedure. Preheat the grill, with the lid closed, to 250° F.

4. Drain the turkey thighs and discard the brine. Rinse under cold running water and pat dry with paper towels. Gently lift the skin of each thigh and push 2 teaspoons of butter underneath. Top the butter with a sage leaf, smoothing it out so it lays flat under the skin. Rub the outside of the skin with more butter. Lightly season with salt and pepper.

5. Place the turkey thighs on the grate at an angle to the bars. Smoke for 1½ hours. Raise the temperature to 375°F (191°C) and roast until the skin is golden brown and the internal temperature in the thickest part of the meat reaches 170°F (77°C), about 30 to 45 minutes.

6. Transfer the thighs to a platter. Let rest for 3 minutes before serving.

Smoked Turkey Jerky

Servings: 6

Cooking Time: 240 Minutes

Ingredients:

- 1/2 Cup soy sauce
- 1/4 Cup water
- 2 Tablespoon honey
- 2 Tablespoon Asian chili garlic sauce
- 2 Tablespoon lime juice
- 1 Tablespoon Morton Tender Quick Home Meat Cure
- 2 Pound (4-5 lb) boneless turkey breast

Directions:

1. In a mixing bowl, combine the soy sauce, water, honey, chili-garlic paste, lime juice, and curing salt, if using. With a sharp knife, slice the turkey into 1/4" thick slices with the grain, which helps it hold together better as it dries. (This is easier if the meat is partially frozen.) Trim any fat, membrane, or connective tissue.

2. Put the turkey slices in a large resealable plastic bag. Pour the marinade mixture over the turkey, and massage the bag so that all the slices get coated with the marinade. Seal the bag and refrigerate for several hours, or overnight.

3. Supply your smoker with wood pellets and follow the start-up procedure. Preheat the grill, with the lid closed, to 180° F.

4. Remove the turkey from the marinade and discard the marinade. Dry the turkey slices between paper towels. Arrange in a single layer directly on the grill grate.

5. Smoke for 2 to 4 hours, or until the jerky is dry but still chewy and somewhat pliant when you bend a piece. Grill: 180 ˚F

6. Transfer to a resealable plastic bag while the jerky's still warm. Let the jerky rest for an hour at room temperature. Squeeze any air from the bag, and refrigerate the jerky. It will keep for several weeks. Enjoy!

Bbq Chicken Breasts

Servings: 6
Cooking Time: 25 Minutes

Ingredients:

- 6 boneless, skinless chicken breast
- 1 1/2 Cup Sweet & Heat BBQ Sauce
- salt and pepper
- 1 Tablespoon chopped parsley, for garnish

Directions:

1. Place chicken breasts and 1 cup of Traeger Sweet & Heat BBQ Sauce in a resealable bag or large bowl, and gently turn to cover chicken evenly in the sauce. Marinate in the refrigerator overnight.
2. Supply your smoker with wood pellets and follow the start-up procedure. Preheat the grill, with the lid closed, to 450° F.
3. Remove chicken from marinade and season with salt and pepper.
4. Place chicken directly on the grill grate and cook for 10 minutes on each side flipping once or until internal temperature reaches 150℉.
5. Brush on remaining 1/2 cup of Traeger Sweet & Heat BBQ Sauce while chicken is still on the grill, and continue to cook 5 to 10 minutes longer or until a finished internal temperature of 165℉.
6. Remove chicken from grill and let rest 5 minutes before serving. Sprinkle with chopped parsley. Enjoy!

Smoked Pulled Chicken

Servings: 6
Cooking Time: 65 Minutes

Ingredients:

- To Taste, Ale House Beer Can Chicken Seasoning
- 1 Lb Chicken Breasts, Boneless, Skinless
- 1 Tbsp Cilantro, Chopped
- 1 Tsp Cumin, Ground
- 2 Jalapeños, Chopped
- 2 Tsp Olive Oil
- 1 Bag Tortilla Chips
- 1 Lb White American Cheese, Cubed
- 1 Cup Milk

Directions:

1. Supply your smoker with wood pellets and follow the start-up procedure. Preheat the grill, with the lid open, to 350° F. If using a gas or charcoal grill, preheat to medium heat.
2. Score the chicken, rub with olive oil, then season with Ale House Beer Can Chicken.
3. Transfer the chicken to the grill and cook for 8 to 10 minutes, turning occasionally.
4. Remove chicken from the grill, and reduce the temperature to 225° F. Allow the chicken to rest for 10 minutes, then pull apart with 2 forks. Set aside.
5. While the chicken is resting, heat a cast iron skillet on the grill. Partially open the sear slide, then to the skillet add the cubed cheese, jalapeño, milk, and cumin. Stir occasionally, for 5 minutes, until the cheese melts. Fold in the pulled chicken, then close the lid and allow the dip to smoke for 30 to 45 minutes.
6. Remove from grill and let rest for 5-10 minutes to thicken. Serve warm with fresh cilantro and tortilla chips.

Bbq Turkey Breast With Meat Church Holy Cow

Servings: 8
Cooking Time: 180 Minutes

Ingredients:

- 1 Large boneless, skinless turkey breast
- 1/4 Cup Duke's Mayonnaise
- Meat Church Holy Cow BBQ Rub
- 1/2 Cup honey
- 1/4 Cup Dijon mustard
- 2 Tablespoon Meat Church Holy Cow BBQ Rub

Directions:

1. Rinse off the breast and pat dry. Slather it liberally in mayonnaise, this will act as a binder for the seasoning. Apply Meat Church Holy Cow BBQ Rub generously to all sides.

2. Supply your smoker with wood pellets and follow the start-up procedure. Preheat the grill, with the lid closed, to 275° F.

3. Place the breast directly on the grill grate and cook for 2 to 3 hours, or until the internal temperature reaches 160°F in the thickest part. (The breast will continue to cook another 5° or so after it is removed from the grill.) Grill: 275 °F Probe: 160 °F

4. While the turkey is cooking you can go ahead and prepare your glaze (if using). Mix all glaze ingredients in a small saucepan and bring to a simmer. Reduce by 1/3. Remove from the heat and set aside.

5. Drizzle the glaze on the turkey during the last 15 minutes of the cook. I recommend doing this around 158 - 160°F, internal temperature. (This turkey is also delicious as-is, without the optional glaze.)

6. Remove from the grill and let the turkey breast rest 5 to 10 minutes before slicing. Enjoy!

Grilled Honey Garlic Wings

Servings: 4
Cooking Time: 60 Minutes

Ingredients:

- 2 1/2 Pound chicken wings
- Pork & Poultry Rub
- 4 Tablespoon butter
- 3 Clove garlic, minced
- 1/4 Cup honey
- 1/2 Cup hot sauce
- 1 1/2 Cup blue cheese or ranch dressing

Directions:

1. Start by segmenting the wings into three pieces, cutting through the joints. Discard the wing tips or save them to make a stock.

2. Lay out the remaining pieces on a rimmed baking sheet lined with nonstick foil or parchment paper. Season well with Traeger Pork & Poultry Rub.

3. Supply your smoker with wood pellets and follow the start-up procedure. Preheat the grill, with the lid closed, to 350° F.

4. Place the baking sheet with wings directly on the grill grate and cook for 45 to 50 minutes or until they are no longer pink at the bone. Grill: 350 °F

5. To make the sauce: Melt butter in a small saucepan. Add the garlic and sauté for 2 to 3 minutes. Add in the honey and hot sauce and cook for a few minutes until completely combined. Keep sauce warm while the wings are cooking.

6. After 45 minutes, pour the spicy honey-garlic sauce over the wings, turning with tongs to coat.

7. Place wings back on the grill and cook for an additional 10 to 15 minutes to set the sauce. Grill: 350 ˚F

8. Serve with ranch or blue cheese dressing. Enjoy!

Lemon & Herb Chicken

Servings: 3-4

Cooking Time: 75 Minutes

Ingredients:

- 1 roaster chicken, about 4lb (1.8kg), preferably organic
- 1 large sweet onion, peeled and sliced lengthwise into 8 wedges
- ½ cup chicken stock or broth
- sprigs of fresh rosemary, thyme, parsley, tarragon, or chives (or a mix)
- lemon wedges
- for the butter
- 4 tbsp unsalted butter, at room temperature
- 1 garlic clove, peeled and finely minced
- 2 tbsp chopped fresh herbs, such as rosemary, thyme, parsley, tarragon, or chives (or a mix)
- 2 tsp lemon zest
- 2 tsp freshly squeezed lemon juice
- ½ tsp coarse salt
- ½ tsp freshly ground black pepper

Directions:

1. Supply your smoker with wood pellets and follow the start-up procedure. Preheat the grill, with the lid closed, to 400˚ F.

2. In a small bowl, make the herb butter by combining the ingredients.

3. Place the chicken on a rimmed sheet pan and tuck the lemon rinds from the butter into the main cavity. Rub the outside of the chicken with the herb butter. (Reserve any remainder.) Tuck the wings behind the back and tie the legs together with butcher's twine. Place the onion wedges in a shallow roasting pan to help form a natural rack for the chicken. (Alternatively, place several large carrots, trimmed and peeled, on the bottom of the pan.) Place the chicken on the onion rack. Add the chicken stock and any remaining herbed butter and lemon juice.

4. Place the roasting pan on the grate, roast the chicken for 30 minutes, and then baste with the juices from the bottom of the pan. Baste every 15 minutes until the chicken is golden brown and the internal temperature reaches 165˚F (74˚C), about 45 minutes more.

5. Transfer the chicken to a cutting board and let rest for 10 minutes. Carve the chicken and place the slices on a platter with a deep well. Spoon some of the juices over the chicken. Scatter fresh herbs over the top. Serve with the lemon wedges.

BEEF LAMB AND GAME RECIPES

Smoked Beef Back Ribs

Servings: 6
Cooking Time: 480 Minutes

Ingredients:
- 2 Rack beef back ribs
- 1/2 Cup Beef Rub

Directions:
1. If your butcher has not already done so, remove the thin papery membrane from the bone-side of the ribs by working the tip of a butter knife underneath the membrane over a middle bone. Use paper towels to get a firm grip, then tear the membrane off.
2. Season both sides of ribs with Traeger Beef Rub.
3. Supply your smoker with wood pellets and follow the start-up procedure. Preheat the grill, with the lid closed, to 225° F.
4. Arrange the ribs on the grill grate, bone side down. Cook for 8-10 hours, or until internal temperature reaches 205°F. Grill: 225 °F Probe: 205 °F
5. Remove ribs from grill and let rest, lightly covered for 20 minutes before slicing and serving. Enjoy!

Jalapeño Beef Jerky

Servings: 8
Cooking Time: 240 Minutes

Ingredients:
- 2 jalapeños, stemmed and seeded (or leave seeds in for a hotter jerky)
- 1/4 Cup lime juice
- 1/4 Cup soy sauce
- 4 Tablespoon brown sugar
- 1 Cup Mexican beer
- 2 Tablespoon Morton Tender Quick Home Meat Cure
- 2 Pound beef top or bottom round, sirloin tip, flank steak or wild game

Directions:
1. In a blender or small food processor, combine the jalapeños, lime juice, soy sauce, curing salt and brown sugar and process until the jalapeño is finely chopped. Set aside.
2. With a sharp knife, trim any fat or connective tissue from the meat. Slice the beef into 1/4 inch thick slices against the grain. (This is easier if the meat is partially frozen.)
3. Place the beef slices in a large resealable bag. Transfer jalapeño mixture to the resealable bag and top with beer. Massage the bag so that all the slices get coated with the marinade. Seal and refrigerate for several hours, or overnight.
4. Supply your smoker with wood pellets and follow the start-up procedure. Preheat the grill, with the lid closed, to 180° F.
5. Remove the beef from the marinade and discard the marinade. Dry the beef slices between paper towels. Arrange the meat in a single layer directly on the grill grate. Grill: 180 °F
6. Smoke for 4 to 5 hours, or until the jerky is dry but still chewy and somewhat pliant when you bend a piece. Grill: 180 °F
7. Transfer to a cooling rack and rest for an hour at room temperature.
8. Store in a resealable bag. Squeeze any air from the bag, and refrigerate the jerky. It will keep for several weeks in the fridge.

Baked Maple Venison Sausage Quiche

Servings: 4
Cooking Time: 45 Minutes

Ingredients:
- 2 Pound Venison, ground
- 12 Whole egg
- 16 Ounce Cottage Cheese, fat free
- 1 1/2 Cup Cheese, Colby/Cheddar
- 1 Teaspoon baking powder
- 1 Whole white onion, chopped
- 4 Ounce Green Chiles, canned, chopped

Directions:
1. Cook ground venison in a medium sauté pan over medium high until browned. Drain off excess fat and set venison aside.
2. Whisk eggs in a large mixing bowl. Add remaining ingredients, stirring after each addition. Transfer mixture to one 13x9 pan and one 9x9 pan.
3. Supply your smoker with wood pellets and follow the start-up procedure. Preheat the grill, with the lid closed, to 350° F.
4. Place casserole dish directly on grill grate and cook for 45 minutes or until a knife inserted into the center comes out clean. Let cool 10 minutes before serving. Enjoy!
5. This recipe was provided by Pro Team member Josh and Sarah Bowmar. Access this, and over a thousand other Traeger recipes on the Traeger App.

Garlic Cheese Bacon Burger

Servings: 7
Cooking Time: 16 Minutes

Ingredients:
- 14 Bacon, Strip
- 3 Lbs Chuck Beef, Ground
- 7 Burger Buns
- 4 Cloves Garlic, Minced
- 1 Onion, Chopped
- 1 Tsp Pepper
- 8 Oz Pepper Jack Cheese, Sliced
- 2 Tomato, Sliced

Directions:
1. Supply your smoker with wood pellets and follow the start-up procedure. Preheat the grill, with the lid closed, to 400° F.
2. In a bowl, mix together the ground chuck, garlic, onion, and pepper. Separate the beef mixtures into about 7 equal bundles and form hamburger patties.
3. Brush the grate with oil, then add the patties and grill them on about 5-8 minutes on each side, or until desired doneness.
4. Remove the burgers from the grill. On the bottom half of the burger bun, add two tomato slices, top with a slice of pepper jack cheese, add the patty,
5. Place another slice of cheese on top, add two slices of bacon and top it off with the other half of the burger bun and serve.

Easy Tri Tip Shepherd's Pie

Servings: 4
Cooking Time: 30 Minutes

Ingredients:
- 1 Cup Beef Broth
- 2 Tablespoons Unsalted Butter
- 2 Tablespoons Chophouse Steak Seasoning
- 2 Tablespoons Flour
- 1 Cup Mashed Potatoes, Prepared
- 2 Cups Tri-Tip, Diced

- 2 Cups Mixed Frozen Vegetables, Thawed

Directions:

1. Supply your smoker with wood pellets and follow the start-up procedure. Preheat the grill, with the lid closed, to 350° F.

2. In the sauce pan, add the butter and flour over medium low heat. Cook the flour and butter for about 1 minute, or until the flour smells toasty. Slowly add in the beef broth, whisking constantly. Cook for 5 minutes, or until the gravy is thick, and then add the Chophouse Steak. Set aside.

3. Toss the vegetables and tri-tip with the gravy and divide equally into the ramekins. Top the ramekins with mashed potatoes and grill the shepherd's pies for 10-15 minutes, or until warm all the way through and the filling is bubbling. Remove from the grill and serve immediately.

Traeger Filet Mignon

Servings: 2
Cooking Time: 10 Minutes

Ingredients:

- 1 Teaspoon salt
- 1 Teaspoon pepper
- 2 Clove garlic, minced
- 3 Tablespoon butter, softened
- 2 filet mignon steaks

Directions:

1. In a small bowl, combine salt, pepper, garlic and softened butter. Rub on both sides of filets. Let rest 10 minutes.

2. Supply your smoker with wood pellets and follow the start-up procedure. Preheat the grill, with the lid closed, to 450° F.

3. Place steaks directly on the grill and cook for 5 to 8 minutes on each side, or until the filets reach an internal temperature of 130°F to 135°F for medium-rare. Enjoy! Pro Tip: With filets there will not be much marbling, so look for a rich, red color. Grill: 450 °F Probe: 140 °F

Savory Cheese Steak Rolls With Puff Pastry

Servings: 4
Cooking Time: 25 Minutes

Ingredients:

- 4 oz american or jack cheese, shredded, divided
- 2 tbsp butter
- to taste, chop house steak rub
- to taste, chop house steak rub (for sauce)
- 3 oz cream cheese
- 1 egg, beaten
- 1 tbsp flour
- 1 tbsp flour (for sauce)
- 1 puff pastry sheet, thawed
- 1 lb sandwich steak, shaved/sliced thin
- 1 tbsp vegetable oil
- 1 cup yellow onion, sliced thin
- 2/3 cup milk

Directions:

1. Supply your smoker with wood pellets and follow the start-up procedure. Preheat the grill, with the lid closed, to 400° F. If using a gas or charcoal grill, set it up for medium-high heat. Preheat the griddle to medium flame.

2. Add oil to the griddle, then cook steak for 2 to 3 minutes, turning with a spatula. Add onions, season with Chop House and cook another minute to soften. Transfer steak and onions to a bowl, then set aside to cool.

3. Meanwhile, melt butter in a sauté pan on the griddle. Stir in flour, then cook for 1 minute. Whisk in milk, then add cream cheese, and 2

ounces of shredded cheese. Whisk until smooth, then remove from the griddle to cool slightly. Use half of the sauce in the pastry, and the other half for serving/dipping once baked.

4. Flour your rolling surface, then set the pastry sheet on top of the flour. Roll the pastry sheet into a 10 to 12 inch square, then cut into 4 squares.

5. Spoon cheese sauce on each pastry square, then divide the steak and onion mixture among the pastries. Top each with remaining shredded cheese, brush sides with beaten egg, then fold pastries over, corner to corner. Secure the seams by pressing down with a fork. Brush the top with beaten egg, then place on a sheet tray.

6. Place the sheet tray on the grill and bake for 18 to 20 minutes, until golden. Remove from the grill, cool for 5 minutes, then cut in half and serve warm with cheese sauce.

Flank Steak Breakfast Potato Burrito

Servings: 4
Cooking Time: 30 Minutes

Ingredients:
- 2 avocado
- 1 cup bacon slices, diced
- 2 tbsp butter
- 1 cup cheddar cheese, shredded
- 2 lbs flank steak
- 4 large flour tortillas
- tt hot sauce
- 2 tsp olive oil
- 1/2 cup onion, chopped
- chop house steak rub
- 2 cups potatoes, diced

Directions:

1. Supply your smoker with wood pellets and follow the start-up procedure. Preheat the grill, with the lid closed, to 425° F. If using a gas or charcoal grill, set it up for medium-high heat. Preheat griddle to medium-low flame.

2. Drizzle olive oil over steak, then generously season steak with the   Chop House Steak Rub. Grill steak 3 minutes [depending on thickness of steak] per side for medium-rare. Remove steak from grill and allow the steak to rest for 10 minutes, then thinly slice against the grain. Set aside.

3. Turn off the grill, then place tortillas inside to warm.

4. Add bacon to the griddle and cook for 2 minutes, then add potatoes to bacon and cook for 2 minutes. Add onions, then cook mixture until bacon is crisp, potatoes have browned, and onions are translucent. Set mixture aside.

5. Melt butter on griddle and then cook scrambled eggs. Set aside.

6. To assemble breakfast burritos, sprinkle cheddar cheese on tortillas. Add scrambled egg, sliced steak, potatoes, and sprinkle with more cheese. Wrap tortillas, by folding sides in, then rolling from the bottom up.

7. Serve hot with fresh avocado and hot sauce.

Flavour Bbq Brisket Burnt Ends

Servings: 6-8
Cooking Time: 420 Minutes

Ingredients:
- 1 Brisket Point
- Georgia Style BBQ Sauce (Mustard Base)
- As Needed Chop House Steak Rub

Directions:

1. Supply your smoker with wood pellets and follow the start-up procedure. Preheat the grill, with the lid closed, to 250° F.

2. Place your brisket on the grates, cook for 6 to 7 hours or until the internal temperature reaches 190°F

3. Remove from the grill and cut into 1-inch cubes. Toss brisket cubes with seasoning and your favorite BBQ sauce into a pan.

4. Place the pan in the grill for 2 hours, stirring half-way through.

The Perfect T-bones

Servings: 4
Cooking Time: 30 Minutes

Ingredients:
- 4 (1½- to 2-inch-thick) T-bone steaks
- 2 tablespoons olive oil
- 1 batch Espresso Brisket Rub or Chili-Coffee Rub

Directions:
1. Supply your smoker with wood pellets and follow the start-up procedure. Preheat the grill, with the lid closed, to 500°F.

2. Coat the steaks all over with olive oil and season both sides with the rub. Using your hands, work the rub into the meat.

3. Place the steaks directly on a grill grate and smoke until their internal temperature reaches 135°F for rare, 145°F for medium-rare, and 155°F for well-done. Remove the steaks from the grill and serve hot.

Spatchcocked Quail With Smoked Fruit

Servings: 4
Cooking Time: 60 Minutes

Ingredients:
- 4 quail, spatchcocked
- 2 teaspoons salt
- 2 teaspoons freshly ground black pepper
- 2 teaspoons garlic powder
- 4 ripe peaches or pears
- 4 tablespoons (½ stick) salted butter, softened
- 1 tablespoon sugar
- 1 teaspoon ground cinnamon

Directions:
1. Supply your smoker with wood pellets and follow the start-up procedure. Preheat, with the lid closed, to 225°F.

2. Season the quail all over with the salt, pepper, and garlic powder.

3. Cut the peaches (or pears) in half and remove the pits (or the cores).

4. In a small bowl, combine the butter, sugar, and cinnamon; set aside.

5. Arrange the quail on the grill grate, close the lid, and smoke for about 1 hour, or until a meat thermometer inserted in the thickest part reads 145°F.

6. After the quail has been cooking for about 15 minutes, add the peaches (or pears) to the grill, flesh-side down, and smoke for 30 to 40 minutes.

7. Top the cooked peaches (or pears) with the cinnamon butter and serve alongside the quail.

Mesquite Smoked Brisket

Servings: 8-12
Cooking Time: 720 Minutes

Ingredients:
- 1 (12-pound) full packer brisket
- 2 tablespoons yellow mustard (you can also use soy sauce)
- Salt

- Freshly ground black pepper

Directions:

1. Supply your smoker with wood pellets and follow the start-up procedure. Preheat the grill, with the lid closed, to 225°F.

2. Using a boning knife, carefully remove all but about ½ inch of the large layer of fat covering one side of your brisket.

3. Coat the brisket all over with mustard and season it with salt and pepper.

4. Place the brisket directly on the grill grate and smoke until its internal temperature reaches 160°F and the brisket has formed a dark bark.

5. Pull the brisket from the grill and wrap it completely in aluminum foil or butcher paper.

6. Increase the grill's temperature to 350°F and return the wrapped brisket to it. Continue to cook until its internal temperature reaches 190°F.

7. Transfer the wrapped brisket to a cooler, cover the cooler, and let the brisket rest for 1 or 2 hours.

8. Remove the brisket from the cooler and unwrap it.

9. Separate the brisket point from the flat by cutting along the fat layer, and slice the flat. The point can be saved for burnt ends (see Sweet Heat Burnt Ends), or sliced and served as well.

The Boss Beef Burger

Servings: 10
Cooking Time: 85 Minutes

Ingredients:

- 4 Lbs Beef, Ground
- 1 Loaf Bread, Sourdough Round
- 1/2 Cup Butter
- Condiments (Ketchup, Mustard, Relish, Etc.)
- Lettuce
- 3 Cups Mushroom
- 3 Onion, Chopped
- Kansas City BBQ Sauce
- Mandarin Habanero Spice
- 1 Lbs Pork, Ground
- Red Onion, Chopped
- 1 Bag Shredded Cheddar Cheese
- Tomato, Sliced

Directions:

1. Supply your smoker with wood pellets and follow the start-up procedure. Preheat the grill, with the lid closed, to 300° F.

2. In a large bowl, mix together the ground beef, ground pork, eggs, barbecue sauce, and seasoning until combined. Do not over mix as this will cause the meat to be tough after cooking. Split the mixture into two equal parts.

3. Melt the butter in a pan over medium heat and sauté the onion mushrooms until golden.

4. In a cast iron pan, flatten one half of the meat mixture into the bottom, taking care to work meat slightly up the sides of the pan. Sprinkle in half of the bag of cheese. Pour in onion mixture and top with the rest of the cheese.

5. On a clean work surface, mold the second half of the meat mixture into a circle and cover the filling to complete the burger. Make sure that the top and bottom meat patties are secured together so that the filling cannot be seen.

6. Place the cast iron pan in the Grill for 1 hour - 1 hour 15 minutes, or until the internal temperature reaches 160°F. Crank up the to "HIGH" and open the flame broiler. Flip the burger out of the cast iron pan onto the grates and sear each side for 5 minutes, to get those beautiful grill marks.

7. To serve: You can make an enormous burger like we did, or you can cut it like a pie into slices to be served on regular hamburger buns with your desired condiments.

Grilled Bacon-wrapped Hot Dogs

Servings: 8
Cooking Time: 20 Minutes

Ingredients:
- 12 Whole hot dogs
- 8 Ounce Cheese, Colby/Cheddar
- 12 Bacon, sliced
- 12 hot dog buns

Directions:
1. Slice the cheese into 8 long strips. Slice the hot dogs lengthwise, leaving a "hinge" on one side, and tuck a piece of cheese into each.
2. Wrap a slice of bacon in a spiral fashion around each hot dog and secure with toothpicks.
3. Supply your smoker with wood pellets and follow the start-up procedure. Preheat the grill, with the lid closed, to 350° F.
4. Arrange the bacon-wrapped hot dogs on the grill grate and cook for 20 to 30 minutes, or until the cheese is melted and the bacon has crisped up. Grill: 350 ˚F
5. Transfer to the buns and serve immediately with your favorite condiments. Enjoy!

Grilled Bell Pepper Flank Steak Fajitas

Servings: 1
Cooking Time: 30 Minutes

Ingredients:
- 1 Green Bell Pepper, Sliced
- 3 Tbsp Olive Oil
- 1 Onion, Diced
- Sweet Heat Rub
- 1 Red Bell Peppers, Sliced
- 1 -16Oz Steak, Flank
- 8 Tortilla, Corn
- 1 Yellow Bell Pepper, Sliced

Directions:
1. Rub flank steak with 1 tbsp olive oil and Sweet Heat Rub Grill seasoning. Cover and marinate in the refrigerator for 1 hour.
2. Lightly brush peppers and onion with olive oil.
3. Supply your smoker with wood pellets and follow the start-up procedure. Preheat the grill, with the lid closed, to 400° F. Place pepper and onion on grill and cook 5 minutes per side. Watch carefully to ensure the peppers and onion do not burn.
4. Remove peppers and onion from grill and toss lightly with remaining olive oil in a medium sized bowl. Transfer peppers and onions to a cutting board and slice into strips. Set aside.
5. Place flank steak directly on grill. Cook until medium rare (an internal temperature of 165°F).
6. Remove flank steak from the grill and transfer to cutting board. Let meat rest for 5 minutes, then slice against the grain into strips.
7. Place flank steak, peppers, and onions in a platter and serve immediately with warm tortillas, salsa, guacamole, sour cream, shredded cheese, thinly sliced iceberg lettuce, or your favorite fajita toppings.

Smoked Chuck Roast Tater Tot Casserole

Servings: 6
Cooking Time: 635 Minutes

Ingredients:

- 2 cups beef stock, divided
- 1 cup cheddar cheese, shredded
- 2 lbs chuck roast
- 1 tbsp cilantro, chopped
- 1 tsp cumin, ground
- 2 jalapeños, chopped
- to taste, lone star brisket rub
- 14 oz tater tots, miniature
- 1 lb white American cheese, cubed
- 1 yellow onion
- 1 cup milk

Directions:

1. Supply your smoker with wood pellets and follow the start-up procedure. Preheat the grill, with the lid closed, to 225° F. If using a gas or charcoal grill, set it up for low, indirect heat.

2. Set the chuck roast on a sheet tray, then season with Lonestar Brisket.

3. Place the chuck roast directly on the grill grate. Close the lid and smoke for 3 hours, spraying with ½ cup of beef stock after the 1st and 2nd hours.

4. Slice the onion and place in a cast iron skillet/Dutch oven with a lid, or aluminum pan. Pour the remaining 1 ½ cups of stock over the onions and set roast on top of onions.

5. Increase the temperature to 275° F and cook an additional 2 ½ to 3 hours, or until internal temperature reaches 165° F.

6. Once 165 F internal temperature is reached, cover the roast with a lid or aluminum foil, and cook another 2 ½ to 3 hours, or until the internal temperature reaches 200° F.

7. Remove the lid then pull the chuck roast apart with tongs. Remove from the grill and set aside.

8. Heat another cast iron skillet on the grill. Open the sear slide, then to the skillet add the cubed cheese, milk, jalapeño, milk, cumin, and cilantro. Stir occasionally, for 5 minutes, until the cheese melts. Close the lid and allow the cheese to smoke for 30 to 45 minutes, then remove from the grill and set aside for casserole assembly.

9. Assemble the casserole: In a deep cast iron skillet, layer the smoked chuck roast, smoked queso, and tater tots.

10. Increase the temperature of the grill to 375° F. If using a gas or charcoal grill, set it to medium heat.

11. Place the skillet on the grill, over indirect heat. Bake for 25 to 30 min, until tater tots begin to brown. Add shredded cheese, then continue baking on the grill for 5 minutes, until the cheese has melted.

12. Remove the casserole from the grill, rest for 10 minutes, then serve warm with additional cilantro, if desired.

Cheesy French Dip Sliders

Servings: 8 - 12
Cooking Time: 60 Minutes

Ingredients:

- 1 ¾ cup beef stock
- 3 lbs. beef top round roast, boneless
- 1 tbsp olive oil
- 2 tbsp chop house steak rub
- 1 8 oz. block of provolone cheese
- 1 red onion, sliced thinly
- ¼ cup sherry

- 1 dozen slider rolls, sliced

Directions:

1. Supply your smoker with wood pellets and follow the start-up procedure. Preheat the grill, with the lid closed, to 400° F.If using a gas or charcoal grill, set it up for medium-high heat.

2. Rub roast with olive oil, then season with Chop House Steak Rub.

3. Place red onion in the bottom of a cast iron skillet and set roast on top. Transfer to grill and roast for 15 minutes. Reduce grill temperature to 325°F then add beef stock and sherry, and continue to cook another 30 minutes, or until 125 to 130°F internal temperature is reached.

4. Remove from grill and allow the roast to rest for 10 minutes, then slice thinly.

5. Assemble sliders on sheet tray by placing sliced beef on the bottom half of each roll. Top with onion and provolone cheese, then place top half of roll on top of cheese. Transfer jus into a metal gravy boat or porcelain ramekin and reserve for serving.

6. Transfer rolls back into cast iron skillet and return to grill for 5 minutes, until cheese melts. Serve hot with jus for dipping

Smoked Texas Bbq Brisket

Servings: 8

Cooking Time: 600 Minutes

Ingredients:

- 1 (14-18 lb) whole packer brisket
- Meat Church Holy Cow BBQ Rub
- Meat Church Holy Gospel BBQ Rub

Directions:

1. Trim any hard fat from all sides of the brisket, being careful not to dig too deep into the meat.

Trim the sides of any excess or loose fat. Trim the fat side of the brisket to 1/4 inch thick.

2. Season all sides evenly with Meat Church Holy Cow Rub. Optionally add a light layer of Meat Church Holy Gospel Rub. Let the brisket sit in the seasoning at room temp for 20 to 30 minutes.

3. Supply your smoker with wood pellets and follow the start-up procedure. Preheat the grill, with the lid closed, to 275° F.

4. Place the brisket fat side up on the grill grate. Cook until it reaches an internal temperature of 165°F, about 5 to 6 hours

5. Remove brisket and wrap tightly in Traeger Butcher Paper.

6. Place the wrapped brisket back on the grill and cook until it reaches an internal temperature of 204°F, about 3-4 hours. Grill: 275 °F Probe: 204 °F

7. When the brisket reaches 204°F, remove from grill and let rest for 30 minutes. When ready to eat, unwrap brisket and slice against the grain. Enjoy!

Korean Style Bbq Prime Ribs

Servings: 5

Cooking Time: 480 Minutes

Ingredients:

- 3 lbs beef short ribs
- 2 tbsp sugar
- 3/4 cup water
- 1 tbsp ground black pepper
- 3 tbsp white vinegar
- 2 tbsp sesame oil
- 3 tbsp soy sauce
- 6 cloves garlic, minced
- 1/3 cup light brown sugar

- 1/2 yellow onion, finely chopped

Directions:

1. Combine soy sauce, water, and vinegar in a bowl. Mix and whisk in brown sugar, white sugar, pepper, sesame oil, garlic, and onion. Whisk until the sugars have completely dissolved

2. Pour marinade into large bowl or baking pan with high sides. Dunk the short ribs in the marinade, coating completely. Cover marinaded short ribs with plastic wrap and refrigerate for 6 to 12 hours3. Preheat pellet grill to 225°F.

3. Remove plastic wrap from ribs and pull ribs out of marinade. Shake off any excess marinade and dispose of the contents left in the bowl.

4. Place ribs on grill and cook for about 6-8 hours, until ribs reach an internal temperature of 203°F. Measure using a probe meat thermometer

5. Once ribs reach temperature, remove from grill and allow to rest for about 20 minutes. Slice, serve, and enjoy!

Salt-crusted Prime Rib

Servings: 8
Cooking Time: 180 Minutes

Ingredients:

- 1 1/2 Cup Jacobsen Salt Co. Pure Kosher Sea Salt
- 3/4 Cup coarse ground black pepper
- 1 Head garlic, peeled
- 1/2 Cup rosemary
- 2 Tablespoon chile powder
- 3/4 Cup extra-virgin olive oil
- 1 (15-16 lb) 6-bone prime rib roast

Directions:

1. In a food processor, combine salt, pepper, garlic cloves, rosemary and chile powder and process until fine. Add the olive oil and pulse to form a paste.

2. Place the prime rib roast on a cutting board, bone-side up and rub with 1 tablespoon of the salt paste.

3. Transfer the meat to a large roasting pan and place bone-side down. Pack the salt paste all over the fatty surface, pressing to help it adhere. Let the prime rib stand at room temperature for 1 hour.

4. Supply your smoker with wood pellets and follow the start-up procedure. Preheat the grill, with the lid closed, to 450° F.

5. Roast the prime rib for 1 hour, or until the crust is slightly darkened. Lower the Traeger temperature to 300°F and roast for about 2 hours and 15 minutes longer, or until an instant-read thermometer inserted into the center of the roast (not touching the bone) registers 125°F for medium-rare. Grill: 450 °F

6. Transfer the roast to a large carving board and let the meat rest for 30 minutes. Grill: 300 °F Probe: 135 °F

7. Carefully lift the salt crust off the meat and transfer to a bowl. Brush away any excess salt.

8. To remove the roast in one piece while keeping the rib rack intact, run a long sharp carving knife along the bones, using them as your guide. Leave on 1/2 inch of meat, or more if reserving for leftovers.

9. Carve the prime rib roast 1/2 inch thick and serve, using some of the crumbled salt crust as a condiment.

Baked Ziti With Italian Sausage

Servings: 6

Cooking Time: 20 Minutes

Ingredients:

- 1 Pound Ziti, cooked 1 minute less than directions, and dried
- 1 Jar Spaghetti Sauce
- 1 Teaspoon garlic, minced
- 1 Pinch red pepper flakes
- 1 Pound Italian Sausage, cooked
- salt and pepper
- 2 Cup Mozzarella Cheese, Grated
- 1/4 Cup Parmesan cheese

Directions:

1. Supply your smoker with wood pellets and follow the start-up procedure. Preheat the grill, with the lid closed, to 450° F.

2. In a large bowl, pour your spaghetti sauce over the cooked pasta, add garlic, red pepper flakes, and salt and pepper to taste. Toss. Fold the sausage into the pasta mixture.

3. Coat a 9 x 13 x 2-inch baking dish with nonstick cooking spray.

4. Pour half of the pasta mixture into your prepared baking dish. Sprinkle with half of the mozzarella. Pour remaining pasta into the dish, smooth out the top and add the remaining mozzarella.

5. Bake in Traeger until cheese is golden brown and bubbly, about 20 minutes.

6. Remove and sprinkle with parmesan cheese. Enjoy!

Green Bell Pepper Cheese Steak Burger

Servings: 4

Cooking Time: 30 Minutes

Ingredients:

- 4 Burger Buns
- 1 Green Bell Pepper, Sliced
- 1 Pound Ground Beef
- 1 Tablespoon Olive Oil
- 1 Tablespoon Chop House Steak Seasoning
- 4 Provolone Cheese, Sliced

Directions:

1. In a large bowl, mix the ground beef and Chop House Steal seasoning together until well combined. Form into patties. Supply your smoker with wood pellets and follow the start-up procedure. Preheat the grill, with the lid closed, to 350° F and grill for 5-7 minutes, flipping halfway through. Once you flip the burgers, top with a slice of provolone cheese.

2. Once the burgers have cooked to your desired degree of doneness, remove from the grill and set aside.

3. For the pepper and onion: in a sauté pan over medium heat, heat the olive oil until it shimmers, then add the onion and pepper. Cook until the pepper and onion are soft and start to caramelize and develop a little char, about 15 minutes.

Roasted Venison Steaks By The Bowmars

Servings: 4

Cooking Time: 25 Minutes

Ingredients:

- 10 Whole Venison Steaks, 6oz
- 1 L Diet Sprite
- 6 Ounce Big Game Rub
- 2 Pound asparagus
- 3 Tablespoon Rub

Directions:

1. The night before, marinade the steaks with sprite and big game rub.

2. Supply your smoker with wood pellets and follow the start-up procedure. Preheat the grill, with the lid closed, to 350° F.

3. Remove steaks from marinade and pat dry. Place steaks directly on the grill grate and cook 10-15 minutes flipping once until the internal temperature reaches 125 degrees for medium rare. Grill: 350 °F

4. Sprinkle asparagus with Traeger Rub and add to Traeger. Cook for 10 minutes turning once.

5. Let steaks rest ten minutes before serving. Enjoy!

Savory Bacon Wrapped Hot Dogs

Servings: 6
Cooking Time: 10 Minutes

Ingredients:

- 1 - 2 Green Bell Pepper, Diced
- 1 Per Hot Dog Bacon, Strip
- 6 - 8 Hot Dog Bun(S)
- 6 - 8 Hot Dog(S)
- Smoke Infused Applewood Bacon Rub
- 2 Tbsp Vegetable Oil

Directions:

1. Supply your smoker with wood pellets and follow the start-up procedure. Preheat the grill, with the lid closed, to 400° F. Before placing anything on the grill, generously oil the cooking grids, using a cloth and vegetable oil.

2. Heat your grill to medium-high heat.

3. Lay a slice of bacon on a cutting board.

4. Roll the bacon and hot dog around until the bacon covers the whole hot dog. Secure with a toothpick on each end.

5. Repeat steps 3 and 4 again, by wrapping each hot dog with one strip of bacon, and secure with a toothpick on each end.

6. Cook the bacon wrapped hot dogs on the grill. When the bacon is lightly crisp, remove from the heat. This takes about 4-6 minutes.

7. Toast the buns by turning the grill up to high. Open the flame broiler. Place bun face down on cooking grids. Toast until desired done.

8. As soon as the hot dogs are done, place them on a toasted bun, pile on the chopped green peppers, and serve.

Grass-fed Beef Burgers

Servings: 4
Cooking Time: 30 Minutes

Ingredients:

- 2 Pound grass-fed ground beef
- 4 Teaspoon kosher salt
- 4 Slices provolone cheese
- 4 brioche burger buns
- 4 Slices Tomato
- Burger Toppings Of Your Choice

Directions:

1. Divide grassfed beef into four portions. To not overwork the meat, remove from the package and directly shape into burger patties about 5" (12cm) across- do not knead the meat. Sprinkle each burger with one teaspoon Kosher salt divided one half on each side.

2. Supply your smoker with wood pellets and follow the start-up procedure. Preheat the grill, with the lid closed, to 415° F.

3. Lay the hamburgers on the grill grate. Cook for 12 minutes for medium rarer- the exterior should be nicely browned. Thermometer should

be placed into the center of the burger and should register 130°F(55 C). Grill: 415 °F Probe: 130 °F

4. During the last few minutes of cooking, add provolone slices to burgers and place buns on the grill to toast. Serve with condiments. Enjoy!

Three Ingredient Pot Roast

Servings: 4

Cooking Time: 180 Minutes

Ingredients:

- 4 Pound chuck roast, cut into 4 inch chunks
- 2 yellow onions, finely sliced
- 2 Teaspoon kosher salt
- 1/4 Cup extra-virgin olive oil
- freshly ground black pepper

Directions:

1. Supply your smoker with wood pellets and follow the start-up procedure. Preheat the grill, with the lid closed, to 400° F.Place half of the chuck roast into a 3-to-4 quart Dutch oven. (Note: if using a roast that is smaller than 4 lbs, make sure to use a smaller Dutch oven as well.)

Add half the onions, half the salt, pepper, and half the olive oil. Repeat with the remaining ingredients.

2. Place a tight-fitting lid on the Dutch oven and place on the grill. Cook for 2 to 3 hours, until the chuck roast can be easily shredded with a fork. Reduce the grill temperature to 350°F if the chuck roast is boiling and not simmering. Grill: 400 °F

3. Remove Dutch oven from the grill and remove the lid. Allow the meat to cool, then skim the fat off the top. Alternatively, allow the meat to cool, refrigerate overnight, then skim the fat cap off the meat before reheating the next day. It will keep for 2 days in the fridge.

4. When ready to serve, this pot roast can be topped with many things to make it your own, including my Preserved Lemon Gremolata, chimichurri, peperonata, horseradish cream (horseradish, sour cream and mayo) or a variety of salsas.

APPETIZERS AND SNACKS

Chicken Wings With Teriyaki Glaze

Servings: 4
Cooking Time: 50 Minutes

Ingredients:

- 16 large chicken wings, about 3lb (1.4kg) total
- 1 to 1½ tbsp toasted sesame oil
- for the glaze
- ½ cup light soy sauce or tamari
- ¼ cup sake or sugar-free dark-colored soda
- ¼ cup light brown sugar or low-carb substitute
- 2 tbsp mirin or 1 tbsp honey
- 1 garlic clove, peeled, minced or grated
- 2 tsp minced fresh ginger
- 1 tsp cornstarch mixed with 1 tbsp distilled water (optional)
- for serving
- 1 tbsp toasted sesame seeds
- 2 scallions, trimmed, white and green parts sliced sharply diagonally

Directions:

1. Supply your smoker with wood pellets and follow the start-up procedure. Preheat the grill, with the lid closed, to 350° F.
2. Place the chicken wings in a large bowl, add the sesame oil, and turn the wings to coat thoroughly.
3. Place the wings on the grate at an angle to the bars. Grill for 20 minutes and then turn. Continue to cook until the wings are nicely browned and the meat is no longer pink at the bone, about 20 minutes more.
4. To make the glaze, in a saucepan on the stovetop over medium-high heat, combine the ingredients and bring the mixture to a boil. Reduce the glaze by 1/3, about 6 to 8 minutes. If you prefer your glaze to be glossy and thick, add the cornstarch and water mixture to the glaze and cook until it coats the back of a spoon, about 1 to 2 minutes more.
5. Transfer the wings to an aluminum foil roasting pan. Pour the glaze over them, turning to coat thoroughly. Place the pan on the grate and cook the wings until the glaze sets, about 5 to 10 minutes.
6. Transfer the wings to a platter. Scatter the sesame seeds and scallions over the top. Serve with plenty of napkins.

Bacon-wrapped Jalapeño Poppers

Servings: 12
Cooking Time: 30 Minutes

Ingredients:

- 8 ounces cream cheese, softened
- ½ cup shredded Cheddar cheese
- ¼ cup chopped scallions
- 1 teaspoon chipotle chile powder or regular chili powder
- 1 teaspoon garlic powder
- 1 teaspoon salt
- 18 large jalapeño peppers, stemmed, seeded, and halved lengthwise
- 1 pound bacon (precooked works well)

Directions:

1. Supply your smoker with wood pellets and follow the start-up procedure. Preheat, with the

lid closed, to 350°F. Line a baking sheet with aluminum foil.

2. In a small bowl, combine the cream cheese, Cheddar cheese, scallions, chipotle powder, garlic powder, and salt.

3. Stuff the jalapeño halves with the cheese mixture.

4. Cut the bacon into pieces big enough to wrap around the stuffed pepper halves.

5. Wrap the bacon around the peppers and place on the prepared baking sheet.

6. Put the baking sheet on the grill grate, close the lid, and smoke the peppers for 30 minutes, or until the cheese is melted and the bacon is cooked through and crisp.

7. Let the jalapeño poppers cool for 3 to 5 minutes. Serve warm.

Bacon Pork Pinwheels (kansas Lollipops)

Servings: 4-6
Cooking Time: 20 Minutes

Ingredients:
- 1 Whole Pork Loin, boneless
- To Taste salt and pepper
- To Taste Greek Seasoning
- 4 Slices bacon
- To Taste The Ultimate BBQ Sauce

Directions:
1. When ready to cook, start the smoker and set temperature to 500F. Preheat, lid closed, for 10 to 15 minutes.

2. Trim pork loin of any unwanted silver skin or fat. Using a sharp knife, cut pork loin length wise, into 4 long strips.

3. Lay pork flat, then season with salt, pepper and Cavender's Greek Seasoning.

4. Flip the pork strips over and layer bacon on unseasoned side. Begin tightly rolling the pork strips, with bacon being rolled up on the inside.

5. Secure a skewer all the way through each pork roll to secure it in place. Set the pork rolls down on grill and cook for 15 minutes.

6. Brush BBQ Sauce over the pork. Turn each skewer over, then coat the other side. Let pork cook for another 5-10 minutes, depending on thickness of your pork. Enjoy!

Bayou Wings With Cajun Rémoulade

Servings: 8
Cooking Time: 40 Minutes

Ingredients:
- 16 large whole chicken wings or 32 drumettes and flats, about 3lb (1.4kg) total
- for the rub
- 1 tbsp kosher salt
- 1 tsp freshly ground black pepper
- 1 tsp paprika
- ½ tsp ground cayenne, plus more
- ½ tsp garlic powder
- ½ tsp celery salt
- ½ tsp dried thyme
- 2 tbsp vegetable oil
- for the rémoulade
- 1¼ cups reduced-fat mayo
- ¼ cup Creole-style or whole grain mustard
- 2 tbsp horseradish
- 2 tbsp pickle relish
- 1 tbsp freshly squeezed lemon juice
- 1 tsp paprika, plus more
- 1 tsp hot sauce, plus more
- 1 tsp Worcestershire sauce
- coarse salt

- for serving
- lemon wedges
- pickled okra (optional)

Directions:

1. Supply your smoker with wood pellets and follow the start-up procedure. Preheat the grill, with the lid closed, to 350° F.

2. If using whole wings, cut through the two joints, separating them into drumettes, flats, and wing tips. (Discard the wing tips or save them for chicken stock.) Alternatively, leave the wings whole. Place the chicken in a resealable plastic bag.

3. In a small bowl, make the rub by combining the ingredients. Mix well. Pour the rub over the wings and toss them to thoroughly coat. Refrigerate for 2 hours.

4. In a small bowl, make the Cajun rémoulade by whisking together the mayo, mustard, horseradish, pickle relish, lemon juice, paprika, hot sauce, and Worcestershire. Season with salt to taste. The mixture should be highly seasoned. Transfer to a serving bowl and lightly dust with paprika. Cover and refrigerate until ready to serve.

5. Remove the wings from the refrigerator and allow the excess marinade to drip off. Place the wings on the grate at an angle to the bars. Grill for 20 minutes and then turn. (They'll brown more evenly but will also have less of a tendency to stick.) Continue to cook until the wings are nicely browned and the meat is no longer pink at the bone, about 20 minutes more.

6. Remove the wings from the grill and pile them on a platter. Serve with the Cajun rémoulade, lemon wedges, and pickled okra (if using).

Pulled Pork Loaded Nachos

Servings: 4

Cooking Time: 10 Minutes

Ingredients:

- 2 cups leftover smoked pulled pork
- 1 small sweet onion, diced
- 1 medium tomato, diced
- 1 jalapeño pepper, seeded and diced
- 1 garlic clove, minced
- 1 teaspoon salt
- 1 teaspoon freshly ground black pepper
- 1 bag tortilla chips
- 1 cup shredded Cheddar cheese
- ½ cup The Ultimate BBQ Sauce, divided
- ½ cup shredded jalapeño Monterey Jack cheese
- Juice of ½ lime
- 1 avocado, halved, pitted, and sliced
- 2 tablespoons sour cream
- 1 tablespoon chopped fresh cilantro

Directions:

1. Supply your smoker with wood pellets and follow the start-up procedure. Preheat, with the lid closed, to 375°F.

2. Heat the pulled pork in the microwave.

3. In a medium bowl, combine the onion, tomato, jalapeño, garlic, salt, and pepper, and set aside.

4. Arrange half of the tortilla chips in a large cast iron skillet. Spread half of the warmed pork on top and cover with the Cheddar cheese. Top with half of the onion-jalapeño mixture, then drizzle with ¼ cup of barbecue sauce.

5. Layer on the remaining tortilla chips, then the remaining pork and the Monterey Jack cheese. Top with the remaining onion-jalapeño mixture

and drizzle with the remaining ¼ cup of barbecue sauce.

6. Place the skillet on the grill, close the lid, and smoke for about 10 minutes, or until the cheese is melted and bubbly. (Watch to make sure your chips don't burn!)

7. Squeeze the lime juice over the nachos, top with the avocado slices and sour cream, and garnish with the cilantro before serving hot.

Citrus-infused Marinated Olives

Servings: 6
Cooking Time: 30 Minutes

Ingredients:

- 1½ cups mixed brined olives, with pits
- ½ cup extra virgin olive oil
- 1 tbsp freshly squeezed lemon juice
- 1 garlic clove, peeled and thinly sliced
- 1 tsp smoked Spanish paprika
- 2 sprigs of fresh rosemary
- 2 sprigs of fresh thyme
- 2 bay leaves, fresh or dried
- 1 small dried red chili pepper, deseeded and flesh crumbled, or ¼ tsp crushed red pepper flakes
- 3 strips of orange zest
- 3 strips of lemon zest

Directions:

1. Supply your smoker with wood pellets and follow the start-up procedure. Preheat the grill, with the lid closed, to 180° F.

2. Drain the olives, reserving 1 tablespoon of brine. Spread the olives in a single layer in an aluminum foil roasting pan. Place the pan on the grate and cook the olives for 30 minutes, stirring the olives or shaking the pan once or twice.

3. In a small saucepan on the stovetop over low heat, warm the olive oil. Whisk in the lemon juice and the reserved 1 tablespoon of brine. Stir in the garlic and paprika. Add the rosemary, thyme, bay leaves, chili pepper, and orange and lemon zests. Warm over low heat for 10 minutes. Remove the saucepan from the heat.

4. Transfer the olives and olive oil mixture to a pint jar. Tuck the aromatics around the sides of the jar. Let cool and then cover and refrigerate for up to 5 days. Let the olives come to room temperature before serving.

Chorizo Queso Fundido

Servings: 4-6
Cooking Time: 20 Minutes

Ingredients:

- 1 poblano chile
- 1 cup chopped queso quesadilla or queso Oaxaca
- 1 cup shredded Monterey Jack cheese
- ¼ cup milk
- 1 tablespoon all-purpose flour
- 2 (4-ounce) links Mexican chorizo sausage, casings removed
- ⅓ cup beer
- 1 tablespoon unsalted butter
- 1 small red onion, chopped
- ½ cup whole kernel corn
- 2 serrano chiles or jalapeño peppers, stemmed, seeded, and coarsely chopped
- 1 tablespoon minced garlic
- 1 tablespoon freshly squeezed lime juice
- 1 teaspoon ground cumin
- 1 teaspoon salt
- 1 teaspoon freshly ground black pepper
- 1 tablespoon chopped fresh cilantro
- 1 tablespoon chopped scallions
- Tortilla chips, for serving

Directions:

1. Supply your smoker with wood pellets and follow the start-up procedure. Preheat, with the lid closed, to 350°F.

2. On the smoker or over medium-high heat on the stove top, place the poblano directly on the grate (or burner) to char for 1 to 2 minutes, turning as needed. Remove from heat and place in a closed-up lunch-size paper bag for 2 minutes to sweat and further loosen the skin.

3. Remove the skin and coarsely chop the poblano, removing the seeds; set aside.

4. In a bowl, combine the queso quesadilla, Monterey Jack, milk, and flour; set aside.

5. On the stove top, in a cast iron skillet over medium heat, cook and crumble the chorizo for about 2 minutes.

6. Transfer the cooked chorizo to a small, grill-safe pan and place over indirect heat on the smoker.

7. Place the cast iron skillet on the preheated grill grate. Pour in the beer and simmer for a few minutes, loosening and stirring in any remaining sausage bits from the pan.

8. Add the butter to the pan, then add the cheese mixture a little at a time, stirring constantly.

9. When the cheese is smooth, stir in the onion, corn, serrano chiles, garlic, lime juice, cuvmin, salt, and pepper. Stir in the reserved chopped charred poblano.

10. Close the lid and smoke for 15 to 20 minutes to infuse the queso with smoke flavor and further cook the vegetables.

11. When the cheese is bubbly, top with the chorizo mixture and garnish with the cilantro and scallions.

12. Serve the chorizo queso fundido hot with tortilla chips.

Grilled Guacamole

Servings: 6
Cooking Time: 30 Minutes

Ingredients:
- 3 large avocados, halved and pitted
- 1 lime, halved
- ½ jalapeño, deseeded and deveined
- ½ small white or red onion, peeled
- 2 garlic cloves, peeled and skewered on a toothpick
- 1 tsp coarse salt, plus more
- 1½ tbsp reduced-fat mayo
- 2 tbsp chopped fresh cilantro
- 2 tbsp crumbled queso fresco (optional)
- tortilla chips

Directions:

1. Supply your smoker with wood pellets and follow the start-up procedure. Preheat the grill, with the lid closed, to 225° F.

2. Place the avocados, lime, jalapeño, and onion cut sides down on the grate. Use the toothpicks to balance the garlic cloves between the bars. Smoke for 30 minutes. (You want the vegetables to retain most of their rawness.)

3. Transfer everything to a cutting board. Remove the garlic cloves from the toothpick and roughly chop. Sprinkle with the salt and continue to mince the garlic until it begins to form a paste. Scrape the garlic and salt into a large bowl.

4. Scoop the avocado flesh from the peels into the bowl. Squeeze the juice of ½ lime over the avocado. Mash the avocados but leave them somewhat chunky. Finely dice the jalapeño. Dice 2 tablespoons of onion. (Reserve the remaining

onion for another use.) Add the jalapeño, onion, mayo, and cilantro to the bowl. Stir gently to combine. Taste for seasoning, adding more salt, lime juice, and jalapeño as desired.

5. Transfer the guacamole to a serving bowl. Top with the queso fresco (if using). Serve with tortilla chips.

Pigs In A Blanket

Servings: 4-6
Cooking Time: 15 Minutes

Ingredients:

- 2 Tablespoon Poppy Seeds
- 1 Tablespoon Dried Minced Onion
- 2 Teaspoon garlic, minced
- 2 Tablespoon Sesame Seeds
- 1 Teaspoon salt
- 8 Ounce Original Crescent Dough
- 1/4 Cup Dijon mustard
- 1 Large egg, beaten

Directions:

1. When ready to cook, start your smoker at 350 degrees F, and preheat with lid closed, 10 to 15 minutes.

2. Mix together poppy seeds, dried minced onion, dried minced garlic, salt and sesame seeds. Set aside.

3. Cut each triangle of crescent roll dough into thirds lengthwise, making 3 small strips from each roll.

4. Brush the dough strips lightly with Dijon mustard. Put the mini hot dogs on 1 end of the dough and roll up.

5. Arrange them, seam side down, on a greased baking pan. Brush with egg wash and sprinkle with seasoning mixture.

6. Bake in smoker until golden brown, about 12 to 15 minutes.

7. Serve with mustard or dipping sauce of your choice. Enjoy!

Simple Cream Cheese Sausage Balls

Servings: 5
Cooking Time: 30 Minutes

Ingredients:

- 1 pound ground hot sausage, uncooked
- 8 ounces cream cheese, softened
- 1 package mini filo dough shells

Directions:

1. Supply your smoker with wood pellets and follow the start-up procedure. Preheat, with the lid closed, to 350°F.

2. In a large bowl, using your hands, thoroughly mix together the sausage and cream cheese until well blended.

3. Place the filo dough shells on a rimmed perforated pizza pan or into a mini muffin tin.

4. Roll the sausage and cheese mixture into 1-inch balls and place into the filo shells.

5. Place the pizza pan or mini muffin tin on the grill, close the lid, and smoke the sausage balls for 30 minutes, or until cooked through and the sausage is no longer pink.

6. Plate and serve warm.

Deviled Eggs With Smoked Paprika

Servings: 6
Cooking Time: 30 Minutes

Ingredients:

* 6 large eggs
* 3 tbsp reduced-fat mayo, plus more
* 1 tsp Dijon or yellow mustard
* ½ tsp Spanish smoked paprika or regular paprika, plus more
* dash of hot sauce
* coarse salt
* freshly ground black pepper
* for garnishing
* small sprigs of fresh parsley, dill, tarragon, or cilantro
* chopped chives
* minced scallions
* Mustard Caviar
* sliced green or black olives
* celery leaves
* sliced radishes
* diced bell peppers
* sliced cherry tomatoes
* fresh or pickled jalapeños
* sliced or diced pickles
* slivers of sun-dried tomatoes
* bacon crumbles
* smoked salmon
* Hawaiian black salt
* Caviar

Directions:

1. Supply your smoker with wood pellets and follow the start-up procedure. Preheat the grill, with the lid closed, to 180° F.

2. On the stovetop over medium-high heat, bring a saucepan of water to a boil. (Make sure there's enough water in the saucepan to cover the eggs by 1 inch [5cm].) Use a slotted spoon to gently lower the eggs into the water. Lower the heat to maintain a simmer. Set a timer for 13 minutes.

3. Prepare an ice bath by combining ice and cold water in a large bowl. Carefully transfer the eggs to the ice bath when the timer goes off.

4. When the eggs are cool enough to handle, gently tap them all over to crack the shell. Carefully peel the eggs. Rinse under cold running water to remove any clinging bits of shell, but don't dry the eggs. (A damp surface will help the smoke adhere to the egg whites.)

5. Place the eggs on the grate and smoke until the eggs take on a light brown patina from the smoke, about 25 minutes. Transfer the eggs to a cutting board, handling them as little as possible.

6. Slice each egg in half lengthwise with a sharp knife. Wipe any yolk off the blade before slicing the next egg. Gently remove the yolks and place them in a food processor. Pulse to break up the yolks. Add the mayo, mustard, paprika, and hot sauce. Season with salt and pepper to taste. Pulse until the filling is smooth. Add additional mayo 1 teaspoon at a time if the mixture is a little dry. (It shouldn't be too loose either.)

7. Spoon the filling into each egg half or pipe it in using a small resealable plastic bag. You can also use a pastry bag fitted with a fluted tip.

8. Place the eggs on a platter and lightly dust with paprika. Accompany with one or more of the suggested garnishes.

Smoked Cashews

Servings: 6

Cooking Time: 60 Minutes

Ingredients:

- 1 pound roasted, salted cashews

Directions:

1. Supply your smoker with wood pellets and follow the start-up procedure. Preheat the grill, with the lid closed, to 120°F.
2. Pour the cashews onto a rimmed baking sheet and smoke for 1 hour, stirring once about halfway through the smoking time.
3. Remove the cashews from the grill, let cool, and store in an airtight container for as long as you can resist.

Pig Pops (sweet-hot Bacon On A Stick)

Servings: 24

Cooking Time: 30 Minutes

Ingredients:

- Nonstick cooking spray, oil, or butter, for greasing
- 2 pounds thick-cut bacon (24 slices)
- 24 metal skewers
- 1 cup packed light brown sugar
- 2 to 3 teaspoons cayenne pepper
- ½ cup maple syrup, divided

Directions:

1. Supply your smoker with wood pellets and follow the start-up procedure. Preheat, with the lid closed, to 350°F.
2. Coat a disposable aluminum foil baking sheet with cooking spray, oil, or butter.
3. Thread each bacon slice onto a metal skewer and place on the prepared baking sheet.
4. In a medium bowl, stir together the brown sugar and cayenne.
5. Baste the top sides of the bacon with ¼ cup of maple syrup.
6. Sprinkle half of the brown sugar mixture over the bacon.
7. Place the baking sheet on the grill, close the lid, and smoke for 15 to 30 minutes.
8. Using tongs, flip the bacon skewers. Baste with the remaining ¼ cup of maple syrup and top with the remaining brown sugar mixture.
9. Continue smoking with the lid closed for 10 to 15 minutes, or until crispy. You can eyeball the bacon and smoke to your desired doneness, but the actual ideal internal temperature for bacon is 155°F
10. Using tongs, carefully remove the bacon skewers from the grill. Let cool completely before handling.

Chuckwagon Beef Jerky

Servings: 6

Cooking Time: 300 Minutes

Ingredients:

- 2½lb (1.2kg) boneless top or bottom round steak, sirloin tip, flank steak, or venison
- 1 cup sugar-free dark-colored soda
- 1 cup cold brewed coffee
- ½ cup light soy sauce
- ¼ cup Worcestershire sauce
- 2 tbsp whiskey (optional)
- 2 tsp chili powder
- 1½ tsp garlic salt
- 1 tsp onion powder
- 1 tsp pink curing salt

Directions:

1. Slice the meat into ¼-inch-thick (.5cm) strips, trimming off any visible fat or gristle. (Slice against the grain for more tender jerky and with the grain for chewier jerky.) Place the meat in a large resealable plastic bag.

2. In a small bowl, whisk together the soda, coffee, soy sauce, Worcestershire sauce, whiskey (if using), chili powder, garlic salt, onion powder, and curing salt (if using). Whisk until the salt dissolves. Pour the mixture over the meat and reseal the bag. Refrigerate for 24 to 48 hours, turning the bag several times to redistribute the brine.

3. Supply your smoker with wood pellets and follow the start-up procedure. Preheat the grill, with the lid closed, to 150° F.

4. Drain the meat and discard the brine. Place the strips of meat in a single layer on paper towels and blot any excess moisture.

5. Place the meat in a single layer on the grate and smoke for 4 to 5 hours, turning once or twice. (If you're aware of hot spots on your grate, rotate the strips so they smoke evenly.) To test for doneness, bend one or two pieces in the middle. They should be dry but still somewhat pliant. Or simply eat a piece to see if it's done to your liking.

6. For the best texture, when you remove the meat from the grill, place the still-warm jerky in a resealable plastic bag and let rest for 30 minutes. (You might see condensation form on the inside of the bag, but the moisture will be reabsorbed by the meat.) Or let the meat cool completely and then store in a resealable plastic bag or covered container. The jerky will last a few days at room temperature but will last longer (up to 2 weeks) if refrigerated.

Smoked Cheese

Servings: 4
Cooking Time: 150 Minutes

Ingredients:

- 1 (2-pound) block medium Cheddar cheese, or your favorite cheese, quartered lengthwise

Directions:

1. Supply your smoker with wood pellets and follow the start-up procedure. Preheat the grill, with the lid closed, to 90°F.

2. Place the cheese directly on the grill grate and smoke for 2 hours, 30 minutes, checking frequently to be sure it's not melting. If the cheese begins to melt, try flipping it. If that doesn't help, remove it from the grill and refrigerate for about 1 hour and then return it to the cold smoker.

3. Remove the cheese, place it in a zip-top bag, and refrigerate overnight.

4. Slice the cheese and serve with crackers, or grate it and use for making a smoked mac and cheese.

Roasted Red Pepper Dip

Servings: 8
Cooking Time: 45 Minutes

Ingredients:

- 4 red bell peppers, halved, destemmed, and deseeded
- 1 cup English walnuts, divided
- 1 small white onion, peeled and coarsely chopped
- 2 garlic cloves, peeled and smashed with a chef's knife
- ¼ cup extra virgin olive oil, plus more
- 1 tbsp balsamic vinegar or balsamic glaze
- 1 tsp honey (eliminate if using balsamic glaze)

- 1 tsp coarse salt, plus more
- 1 tsp ground cumin
- 1 tsp smoked paprika
- ½ to 1 tsp Aleppo red pepper flakes, plus more
- ¼ cup fresh white breadcrumbs (optional)
- distilled water (optional)
- assorted crudités or wedges of pita bread

Directions:

1. Supply your smoker with wood pellets and follow the start-up procedure. Preheat the grill, with the lid closed, to 400° F.

2. Place the peppers skin side down on the grate and grill until the skins blister and the flesh softens, about 30 minutes. Transfer the peppers to a bowl and cover with plastic wrap. Let cool to room temperature. Remove the skins with a paring knife or your fingers. Coarsely chop or tear the peppers.

3. Place ¾ cup of walnuts in an aluminum foil roasting pan. Place the pan on the grate and toast for 10 to 15 minutes, stirring twice. Remove the pan from the grill and let the walnuts cool.

4. Place the peppers, onion, garlic, and walnuts in a food processor fitted with the chopping blade. Pulse several times. Add the olive oil, balsamic vinegar, honey, salt, cumin, paprika, and red pepper flakes. Process until the mixture is fairly smooth. Taste for seasoning, adding more salt or red pepper flakes (if desired). (If the mixture is too loose, add breadcrumbs until the texture is to your liking. If it's too thick, add olive oil or water 1 tablespoon at a time.)

5. Transfer the dip to a serving bowl. Use the back of a spoon to make a shallow depression in the center. Top with the remaining ¼ cup of walnuts and drizzle olive oil in the depression. Serve with crudités or pita bread.

Delicious Deviled Crab Appetizer

Servings: 30
Cooking Time: 10 Minutes

Ingredients:

- Nonstick cooking spray, oil, or butter, for greasing
- 1 cup panko breadcrumbs, divided
- 1 cup canned corn, drained
- ½ cup chopped scallions, divided
- ½ red bell pepper, finely chopped
- 16 ounces jumbo lump crabmeat
- ¾ cup mayonnaise, divided
- 1 egg, beaten
- 1 teaspoon salt
- 1 teaspoon freshly ground black pepper
- 2 teaspoons cayenne pepper, divided
- Juice of 1 lemon

Directions:

1. Supply your smoker with wood pellets and follow the start-up procedure. Preheat, with the lid closed, to 425°F.

2. Spray three 12-cup mini muffin pans with cooking spray and divide ½ cup of the panko between 30 of the muffin cups, pressing into the bottoms and up the sides. (Work in batches, if necessary, depending on the number of pans you have.)

3. In a medium bowl, combine the corn, ¼ cup of scallions, the bell pepper, crabmeat, half of the mayonnaise, the egg, salt, pepper, and 1 teaspoon of cayenne pepper.

4. Gently fold in the remaining ½ cup of breadcrumbs and divide the mixture between the prepared mini muffin cups.

5. Place the pans on the grill grate, close the lid, and smoke for 10 minutes, or until golden brown.

6. In a small bowl, combine the lemon juice and the remaining mayonnaise, scallions, and cayenne pepper to make a sauce.

7. Brush the tops of the mini crab cakes with the sauce and serve hot.

Smoked Turkey Sandwich

Servings: 1

Cooking Time: 15 Minutes

Ingredients:

- 2 slices sourdough bread
- 2 tablespoons butter, at room temperature
- 2 (1-ounce) slices Swiss cheese
- 4 ounces leftover Smoked Turkey
- 1 teaspoon garlic salt

Directions:

1. Supply your smoker with wood pellets and follow the start-up procedure. Preheat the grill, with the lid closed, to 375°F.

2. Coat one side of each bread slice with 1 tablespoon of butter and sprinkle the buttered sides with garlic salt.

3. Place 1 slice of cheese on each unbuttered side of the bread, and then put the turkey on the cheese.

4. Close the sandwich, buttered sides out, and place it directly on the grill grate. Cook for 5 minutes. Flip the sandwich and cook for 5 minutes more. Remove the sandwich from the grill, cut it in half, and serve.

Sriracha & Maple Cashews

Servings: 10

Cooking Time: 60 Minutes

Ingredients:

- 2 tbsp unsalted butter
- 3 tbsp pure maple syrup
- 1 tbsp sriracha
- 1 tsp coarse salt (use only if nuts are unsalted)
- 2½ cups unsalted cashews

Directions:

1. Supply your smoker with wood pellets and follow the start-up procedure. Preheat the grill, with the lid closed, to 250° F.

2. In a small saucepan on the stovetop over low heat, melt the butter. Add the maple syrup, sriracha, and salt (if using). Stir until combined. Add the nuts and stir gently to coat thoroughly.

3. Spread the nuts in a single layer in an aluminum foil roasting pan coated with cooking spray. Place the pan on the grate and smoke the nuts until they're lightly toasted, about 1 hour, stirring once or twice.

4. Remove the pan from the grill and let the nuts cool for 15 minutes. They'll be sticky at first but will crisp up. Break them up with your fingers and store at room temperature in an airtight container, such as a lidded glass jar.

Jalapeño Poppers With Chipotle Sour Cream

Servings: 8

Cooking Time: 45 Minutes

Ingredients:

- 3 strips of thin-sliced bacon
- 12 large jalapeños, red, green, or a mix
- 8oz (225g) light cream cheese, at room temperature
- 1 cup shredded pepper Jack, Monterey Jack, or Cheddar cheese
- 1 tsp chili powder
- ½ tsp garlic salt

- smoked paprika
- for the sour cream
- 1¼ cups light sour cream
- juice of ½ lime
- ½ to 1 canned chipotle peppers in adobo sauce, finely minced, plus 1 tsp of sauce, plus more
- 1 tbsp minced fresh cilantro leaves
- ½ tsp coarse salt, plus more

Directions:

1. Supply your smoker with wood pellets and follow the start-up procedure. Preheat the grill, with the lid closed, to 375° F.

2. Line a rimmed sheet pan with aluminum foil and place a wire rack on top. Place the bacon in a single layer on the wire rack. Place the pan on the grate and grill until the bacon is crisp and golden brown, about 20 minutes. Transfer the bacon to paper towels to cool and then crumble. Set aside.

3. In a small bowl, make the chipotle sour cream by whisking together the ingredients. Add more salt, chipotle peppers, or adobe sauce to taste. Cover and refrigerate.

4. Slice the jalapeños lengthwise through their stems. Scrape out the veins and seeds with the edge of a small metal spoon.

5. In a small bowl, beat together the cream cheese, shredded cheese, chili powder, and garlic salt. Stir in the crumbled bacon. Mound the cream cheese mixture in the jalapeño halves. Line another rimmed sheet pan with aluminum foil and place a wire rack on top. Place the jalapeños filled side up in a single layer on the wire rack.

6. Place the sheet pan on the grate and roast the jalapeños until the filling has melted and the peppers have softened, about 20 to 25 minutes. (They should no longer look bright in color.)

Remove the pan from the grill and let the peppers rest for 5 minutes.

7. Transfer the poppers to a platter and lightly dust with paprika. Serve with the chipotle sour cream.

Cold-smoked Cheese

Servings: 6
Cooking Time: 180 Minutes

Ingredients:

- 2lb (1kg) well-chilled hard or semi-hard cheese, such as:
- Edam
- Gouda
- Cheddar
- Monterey Jack
- pepper Jack
- goat cheese
- fresh mozzarella
- Muenster
- aged Parmigiano-Reggiano
- Gruyère
- blue cheese

Directions:

1. Unwrap the cheese and remove any protective wax or coating. Cut into 4-ounce (110g) portions to increase the surface area.

2. If possible, move your smoker to a shady area. Place 1 resealable plastic bag filled with ice on top of the drip pan. This is especially important on a warm day because you want to keep the interior temperature of the grill between 70 and 90°F (21 and 32°C) or below.

3. Place a grill mat on one side of the grate. Place the cheese on the mat and allow space between each piece.

4. Fill your smoking tube or pellet maze (see Cast Iron Skillets and Grill Pans) with pellets or sawdust and light according to the manufacturer's instructions. Place the smoking tube on the grate near—but not on—the grill mat. When the tube is smoking consistently, close the grill lid.

5. Smoke the cheese for 1 to 3 hours, replacing the pellets or sawdust and ice if necessary. Monitor the temperature and make sure the cheese isn't beginning to melt. Carefully lift the mat with the cheese to a rimmed baking sheet and let the cheese cool completely before handling.

6. Package the smoked cheese in cheese storage paper or bags or vacuum-seal the cheese, labeling each. (While you can wrap the cheese tightly in plastic wrap, the cheese will spoil faster.) Let the cheese rest for at least 2 to 3 days before eating. It will be even better after 2 weeks.

COCKTAILS RECIPES

Smoked Ice Mojito Slurpee

Servings: 2

Cooking Time: 30 Minutes

Ingredients:

- water
- 1 Cup white rum
- 1/2 Cup lime juice
- 1/4 Cup Smoked Simple Syrup
- 12 Whole fresh mint leaves
- 4 Sprig mint
- 4 Whole lime wedge, for garnish

Directions:

1. Supply your smoker with wood pellets and follow the start-up procedure. Preheat the grill, with the lid closed, to 180° F.

2. For optimal flavor, use Super Smoke if available. Grill: 180 ℉

3. Remove water from grill and pour smoked water into ice cube trays. Place in freezer until frozen.

4. Add rum, lime juice, Traeger Smoked Simple Syrup, mint and smoked ice to a blender.

5. Blend until a slushy consistency and pour into glasses.

6. Garnish with a mint sprig and lime wedge. Enjoy!

In Traeger Fashion Cocktail

Servings: 2

Cooking Time: 20 Minutes

Ingredients:

- 2 Whole orange peel
- 2 Whole lemon peel
- 3 Ounce bourbon
- 1 Ounce Smoked Simple Syrup
- 6 Dash Bitters Lab Charred Cedar & Currant Bitters

Directions:

1. Supply your smoker with wood pellets and follow the start-up procedure. Preheat the grill, with the lid closed, to 350° F.

2. Place the lemon and orange peel directly on the grill grate and cook 20 to 25 minutes or until lightly browned. Grill: 350 ℉

3. Add bourbon, Traeger Smoked Simple Syrup and bitters to a mixing glass and stir over ice. Stir until glass is chilled and contents are well diluted.

4. Strain into a new glass over fresh ice and garnish with grilled lemon and orange peel. Enjoy!

Traeger Gin & Tonic

Servings: 2

Cooking Time: 45 Minutes

Ingredients:

- 1/2 Cup berries
- 2 orange, sliced
- 4 Tablespoon granulated sugar
- 3 Ounce gin
- 1 Cup tonic water
- 2 Sprig fresh mint, for garnish

Directions:

1. Supply your smoker with wood pellets and follow the start-up procedure. Preheat the grill, with the lid closed, to 180° F.

2. For the Smoked Berries: Spread mixed fresh berries on a sheet pan and place directly on the grill grate. Smoke for 30 minutes then remove from grill. Grill: 180 ℉

3. For the Orange Slices: Increase the grill temperature to 450℉ and preheat, lid closed for 15 minutes. Grill: 450 ℉

4. Toss the orange slices with granulated sugar and place directly on grill grate. Cook for about 5 minutes, turning once or until the slices have developed grill marks. Grill: 450 ℉

5. Pour gin into a glass, add ice and berries, then top with tonic water. Garnish with a fresh mint sprig and grilled orange wheel. Enjoy!

Grilled Peach Smash Cocktail

Servings: 2
Cooking Time: 10 Minutes

Ingredients:
- 2 peach, sliced and grilled
- 10 fresh mint leaves
- 1 1/2 Ounce Smoked Simple Syrup
- 4 Ounce bourbon
- 2 mint sprig, for garnish

Directions:
1. Supply your smoker with wood pellets and follow the start-up procedure. Preheat the grill, with the lid closed, to 375° F.

2. Cut the peach into 6 slices and brush with Traeger Smoked Simple Syrup. Place directly on the grill grate and cook 10 to 12 minutes or until peaches soften and get grill marks. Grill: 375 ℉

3. In a mixing glass, add 3 slices of grilled peaches, 5 mint leaves and Traeger Smoked Simple Syrup.

4. Muddle ingredients to release oils of the mint and juices from the grilled peaches. Add bourbon and crushed ice.

5. Shake and pour into a stemless wine glass. Top off with more crushed ice. Garnish with a grilled peach and mint sprig. Enjoy!

Honey Glazed Grapefruit Shandy Cocktail

Servings: 2
Cooking Time: 20 Minutes

Ingredients:
- 4 grapefruits
- 4 Tablespoon honey
- granulated sugar
- 2 Ounce bourbon
- 1 Ounce Smoked Simple Syrup
- 4 Ounce honey glazed grilled grapefruit, juiced
- 2 Bottle Ballast Point Grapefruit Sculpin

Directions:
1. Supply your smoker with wood pellets and follow the start-up procedure. Preheat the grill, with the lid closed, to 375° F.

2. For the honey glazed grapefruit: Slice one grapefruit in half and coat with 2 tablespoons honey.

3. Take the other grapefruit and slice into wheels. Toss the wheels in granulated sugar until well coated.

4. Place the grapefruit halves and wheels directly on the grill grate, cut side down, and cook for 20 to 30 minutes. Remove from grill and set the wheels aside. Grill: 375 ℉

5. Squeeze the grapefruit halves into a measuring cup. It should yield about 2 oz juice.

6. Pour the grapefruit juice into a shaker and add bourbon and Traeger Smoked Simple Syrup then top with ice. Shake for 10-15 seconds.

7. Strain into glass, add ice and fill with beer. Garnish with the grilled grapefruit wheel. Enjoy!

Smoky Scotch & Ginger Cocktail

Servings: 2

Cooking Time: 60 Minutes

Ingredients:

- 1 Ounce ginger syrup
- 1/2 Ounce brandied cherry juice
- 1/2 Ounce agave nectar
- 4 Ounce scotch
- 1 1/2 Ounce lemon juice
- 2 Slices grilled lemon, for garnish
- 2 cherry, for garnish

Directions:

1. Supply your smoker with wood pellets and follow the start-up procedure. Preheat the grill, with the lid closed, to 180° F.

2. For the smoked ginger cherry syrup: Place ginger syrup, cherry juice and agave nectar in a shallow dish and place the dish directly on the grill grate.

3. Smoke for 60 minutes, or until the mixture has picked up the smoke flavor. Remove from grill and allow to cool for 30 minutes. Grill: 180 °F

4. Place smoked ginger cherry syrup, scotch and lemon juice into a shaker tin and shake with ice. Strain into a glass over fresh ice and garnish with a grilled lemon wheel and cherry. Enjoy!

Smoked Pumpkin Spice Latte

Servings: 4

Cooking Time: 45 Minutes

Ingredients:

- 1 Small sugar pumpkin
- olive oil
- 1 Can sweetened condensed milk
- 1 Cup whole milk
- 2 Tablespoon Smoked Simple Syrup
- 1 Teaspoon pumpkin pie spice
- pinch of salt
- cinnamon
- whipped cream
- shaved nutmeg
- 8 Ounce smoked cold brew coffee

Directions:

1. Supply your smoker with wood pellets and follow the start-up procedure. Preheat the grill, with the lid closed, to 325° F.

2. Cut the sugar pumpkin in half, scoop out the seeds and discard. Place the pumpkin halves cut side up on a baking sheet and brush lightly with olive oil.

3. Place the sheet tray directly on the grill grate and cook 45 minutes or until the flesh is tender. Remove from heat and place on the counter to cool. Grill: 325 °F

4. When the pumpkin is cool enough to handle, scoop out the flesh and mash until smooth.

5. Place 3 Tbsp of the pumpkin puree in a separate bowl and reserve the remaining for another use.

6. Add the sweetened condensed milk, whole milk, Traeger Smoked Simple Syrup, pumpkin pie seasoning and salt to the pumpkin puree. Whisk to combine.

7. Pour the cold brew over ice, add desired amount of pumpkin spice creamer and top with whipped cream, cinnamon, and shaved nutmeg if desired. Enjoy!

Smoked Hot Buttered Rum

Servings: 4

Cooking Time: 30 Minutes

Ingredients:

- 2 Cup water
- 1/4 Cup brown sugar
- 1/2 Stick butter, melted
- 1 Teaspoon ground cinnamon
- 1/4 Teaspoon ground nutmeg
- ground cloves
- salt
- 6 Ounce Rum

Directions:

1. Supply your smoker with wood pellets and follow the start-up procedure. Preheat the grill, with the lid closed, to 180° F.

2. In a shallow baking dish, combine 2 cups water with all ingredients except for the rum and place directly on the grill grate. Smoke for 30 minutes. Grill: 180 ˚F

3. Remove from the grill and pour into the pitcher of a blender. Process until somewhat frothy.

4. Pour 1.5 ounces of rum each into 4 glasses. Split hot butter mixture evenly between the four glasses.

5. Garnish with a cinnamon stick and freshly grated nutmeg. Enjoy!

Smoked Apple Cider

Servings: 2

Cooking Time: 30 Minutes

Ingredients:

- 32 Ounce apple cider
- 2 cinnamon sticks
- 4 whole cloves
- 3 star anise
- 2 Pieces orange peel
- 2 Pieces lemon peel

Directions:

1. Supply your smoker with wood pellets and follow the start-up procedure. Preheat the grill, with the lid closed, to 225° F.

2. Combine the cider, cinnamon stick, star anise, clove, lemon and orange peel in a shallow baking dish.

3. Place directly on the grill grate and smoke for 30 minutes. Remove from grill, strain and transfer to four mugs. Grill: 225 ˚F

4. Finish with a slice of apple and a cinnamon stick to serve. Enjoy!

Grilled Blood Orange Mimosa

Servings: 4

Cooking Time: 15 Minutes

Ingredients:

- 3 blood orange, halved
- 2 Tablespoon granulated sugar
- 1 Bottle sparkling wine
- thyme sprigs, for garnish

Directions:

1. Supply your smoker with wood pellets and follow the start-up procedure. Preheat the grill, with the lid closed, to 375° F.

2. When the grill is hot, dip the cut side of the orange halves in sugar and place cut side down directly on the grill grate. Grill: 375 ˚F

3. Grill the oranges for 10-15 minutes or until grill marks develop. Grill: 375 ˚F

4. Remove from the grill and let cool at room temperature.

5. When cool enough to handle, juice the oranges and strain through a fine strainer removing any pulp.

6. Pour 5 oz of sparkling wine into each glass and top with 1 oz blood orange juice.

7. Garnish with a sprig of thyme. Enjoy!

Smoked Hibiscus Sparkler

Servings: 4

Cooking Time: 30 Minutes

Ingredients:

- 1/2 Cup sugar
- 2 Tablespoon dried hibiscus flowers
- 1 Bottle sparkling wine
- crystallized ginger, for garnish

Directions:

1. Supply your smoker with wood pellets and follow the start-up procedure. Preheat the grill, with the lid closed, to 180° F.

2. Place water in a shallow baking dish and place directly on the grill grate. Smoke the water for 30 minutes or until desired smoke flavor is achieved. Grill: 180 ˚F

3. Pour water into a small saucepan and add sugar and hibiscus flowers. Bring to a simmer over medium heat and cook until sugar is dissolved.

4. Strain out the hibiscus flowers and transfer your simple syrup to a small container and refrigerate until chilled.

5. Pour 1/2 ounce smoked hibiscus simple syrup in the bottom of a champagne glass and top with sparkling wine.

6. Drop in a few pieces of crystallized ginger to garnish. Enjoy!

Smoky Mountain Bramble Cocktail

Servings: 2

Cooking Time: 15 Minutes

Ingredients:

- 16 Ounce blackberries
- 2 Cup sugar
- 10 smoked blackberries
- 3 Ounce vodka
- 1 1/2 Ounce Alpine Distilling Preserve Liqueur
- 1 1/2 Ounce lemon juice
- 1 Ounce smoked blackberry syrup

Directions:

1. Supply your smoker with wood pellets and follow the start-up procedure. Preheat the grill, with the lid closed, to 180° F.

2. To make Smoked Blackberry Simple Syrup: Place blackberries on a grill mat and smoke for 15 to 20 minutes. Grill: 180 ˚F

3. Combine 1 cup water and sugar in a small sauce pan and warm over medium heat until sugar dissolves. Remove from heat and place 2/3 of blackberries in the simple syrup and macerate.

4. Strain through a fine mesh strainer and store for up to 14 days.

5. To make the cocktail: Muddle 4 to 5 smoked blackberries in a cocktail shaker. Add vodka, Preserve Liqueur, lemon and smoked blackberry syrup. Add ice and shake vigorously. Double strain into an old fashioned glass.

6. Garnish with a smoked blackberry and lemon twist. Enjoy!

Smoked Texas Ranch Water

Servings: 4

Cooking Time: 60 Minutes

Ingredients:

- 3 Whole limes
- 1 Tablespoon Blackened Saskatchewan Rub
- 12 Ounce blanco tequila
- 24 Ounce Topo Chico or other sparkling mineral water
- 8 Slices jalapeño, optional

Directions:

1. Supply your smoker with wood pellets and follow the start-up procedure. Preheat the grill, with the lid closed, to 225° F.

2. Cut two of the limes in half and sprinkle with Traeger Blackened Saskatchewan Rub. Place the four lime halves on the edge of the grill grate and smoke for 1 hour. Remove from grill and set aside to cool. Grill: 225 ℉

3. Pour some of the rub onto a small plate. Cut the third lime into 1/4 wedges and use the lime to rub the rim of 4 cocktail glasses, turn the glasses upside down, and into the rub to salt the rim.

4. Place several ice cubes into your rimmed glasses and pour 3 ounces tequila, 6 ounces Topo Chico, squeeze the juice of one smoked lime (discard after squeezing), and add one fresh lime wedge to each. If using the jalapeño, add one or two slices to each glass (muddle if desired).

5. Stir to combine and enjoy!

Smoked Grape Lime Rickey

Servings: 4

Cooking Time: 45 Minutes

Ingredients:

- 1/2 Pound red grapes
- 1/2 Cup plus 1 tablespoon sugar
- 1/2 Cup water
- 1 limes, sliced
- 2 limes, halved
- 1 Tablespoon sugar
- 1 L lemon lime soda

Directions:

1. Supply your smoker with wood pellets and follow the start-up procedure. Preheat the grill, with the lid closed, to 180° F.

2. Rinse grapes well and place in a shallow baking dish. Combine 1/2 cup sugar and water and stir until sugar dissolves. Pour over grapes.

3. Place the baking dish directly on the grill grate and smoke for 30 to 40 minutes until grapes are tender. Grill: 180 ℉

4. Remove from the grill and pour entire contents of the baking dish in a blender. Puree on high until smooth then pass the mixture through a fine mesh strainer.

5. Increase Traeger temperature to 350℉. Grill: 350 ℉

6. Toss the lime slices and lime halves with 1 tablespoon sugar and place directly on the grill grate. Cook for 15 to 20 minutes or until grill marks develop. Remove from grill and set slices aside. When cool enough to handle, juice grilled lime halves. Grill: 350 ℉

7. To build the drink, fill a pint glass with ice. Pour in 1-1/2 ounce grilled lime juice, 1-1/2 ounce smoked grape syrup and top off with soda. Garnish with grilled lime slice. Enjoy!

Zombie Cocktail Recipe

Servings: 2

Cooking Time: 45 Minutes

Ingredients:
- fresh squeezed orange juice
- pineapple juice
- 2 Ounce light rum
- 2 Ounce dark rum
- 2 Ounce lime juice
- 1 Ounce Smoked Simple Syrup
- 6 Ounce smoked orange and pineapple juice
- 2 grilled orange peel, for garnish
- 2 grilled pineapple chunks, for garnish

Directions:

1. Supply your smoker with wood pellets and follow the start-up procedure. Preheat the grill, with the lid closed, to 180° F.

2. Smoked Orange and Pineapple Juice: Pour equal parts fresh squeezed orange juice and pineapple juice into a shallow sheet pan and smoke for 45 minutes. Remove and let cool. Measure out 3 ounces of juice and reserve any remaining juice in the refrigerator for future use. Grill: 180 °F

3. Add dark and light rums, 3 ounces smoked orange and pineapple juice, lime juice and Traeger Smoked Simple Syrup to a mixing glass.

4. Add ice, shake and strain over clean ice into a Tiki glass.

5. Garnish with a grilled orange peel and grilled pineapple. Enjoy!

Smoked Irish Coffee

Servings: 2

Cooking Time: 15 Minutes

Ingredients:
- 10 Ounce hot coffee
- 1/2 Cup heavy cream
- 1 Tablespoon sugar
- 2 Ounce Irish whiskey
- freshly grated nutmeg, for garnish (optional)

Directions:

1. Supply your smoker with wood pellets and follow the start-up procedure. Preheat the grill, with the lid closed, to 180° F.

2. Place the coffee and cream in separate shallow baking dishes and place both directly on the grill grate. Smoke for 10 to 15 minutes until the liquids pick up a slight smoke flavor. Grill: 180 °F

3. Remove from the grill and cool the cream. When the cream is cool, add sugar and whip in a stand mixer or by hand to soft peaks.

4. Pour the hot coffee into two mugs then add 2 ounces of whiskey to each.

5. Top with smoked whipped cream and finish with freshly grated nutmeg, if desired. Enjoy!

Bacon Old-fashioned Cocktail

Servings: 2

Cooking Time: 20 Minutes

Ingredients:
- 16 Slices bacon
- 1/2 Cup warm water (110°F to 115°F)
- 1500 mL bourbon
- 1/2 Fluid Ounce maple syrup
- 4 Dash Angostura bitters
- 2 fresh orange peel

Directions:

1. Smoke bacon prior to making Old Fashioned using this recipe for Applewood Smoked Bacon.

2. To Make Bacon: Supply your smoker with wood pellets and follow the start-up procedure. Preheat the grill, with the lid closed, to 325° F.

3. Place bacon in a single layer on a cooling rack that fits inside a baking sheet pan. Cook in Traeger for 15-20 minutes or until bacon is browned and crispy. Reserve bacon for later. Let the fat cool slightly; you'll use the fat to infuse the bourbon. Grill: 325 °F

4. Combine 1/4 cup of warm (not hot) liquid bacon fat with the entire contents of a 750ml bottle of bourbon in a glass or heavy plastic container.

5. Use a fork to stir well. Let it sit on the counter for a few hours, stirring every so often.

6. After about four hours, put bourbon fat mixture into the freezer. After about an hour, the fat will congeal and you can simply scoop it out with a spoon. You can fine-strain the mixture through a sieve to remove all fat if desired.

7. Combine ingredients with ice and stir until cold. Strain over fresh ice in an Old Fashioned glass and garnish with reserved bacon and orange peel. Enjoy!

Smoked Eggnog

Servings: 4
Cooking Time: 60 Minutes

Ingredients:
- 2 Cup whole milk
- 1 Cup heavy cream
- 4 egg yolk
- Cup sugar
- 3 Ounce bourbon
- 1 Teaspoon vanilla extract
- 1 Teaspoon nutmeg
- 4 egg white
- whipped cream

Directions:
1. Plan ahead, this recipe requires chill time.

2. Supply your smoker with wood pellets and follow the start-up procedure. Preheat the grill, with the lid closed, to 180° F.

3. Pour the milk and the cream into a baking pan and smoke on the Traeger for 60 minutes. Grill: 180 °F

4. Meanwhile, in the bowl of a stand mixer, beat the egg yolks until they lighten in color. Gradually add 1/3 cup sugar and continue to beat until sugar completely dissolves.

5. After the milk and cream have smoked, add them along with the bourbon, vanilla and nutmeg into the egg mixture and stir to combine.

6. Place the egg whites in the bowl of a stand mixer and beat to soft peaks. When you lift the beaters the whites will make a peak that slightly curls down.

7. With the mixer still running, gradually add 1 tablespoon of sugar and beat until stiff peaks form.

8. Gently fold the egg whites into the cream mixture and then whisk to thoroughly combine.

9. Chill eggnog for a couple hours to let the flavors meld. Garnish with a dash of nutmeg and whipped cream on top. Enjoy!

Grilled Rabbit Tail Cocktail

Servings: 2
Cooking Time: 25 Minutes

Ingredients:
- 1 1/2 Ounce lemon juice
- 4 Ounce Apple Brandy
- 1 Ounce orange juice
- 1 Ounce Smoked Simple Syrup

Directions:
1. Supply your smoker with wood pellets and follow the start-up procedure. Preheat the grill, with the lid closed, to 350° F.

2. Place lemon halves directly on the grill grate and cook for 20-25 minutes or until grill marks appear. Remove from grill and let cool. Once cool enough to handle, juice the lemons then chill and reserve the juice. Grill: 350 ˚F

3. Using the proportions listed above and considering the size and consumption rate of your tailgate crew or party, mix all the above ingredients in a large thermos and top with a bit of ice.

4. Using 6-8 oz glasses or cups, guests can serve themselves from the thermos and garnish each drink with a grilled apple slice. Enjoy!

Grilled Peach Mint Julep

Servings: 2

Cooking Time: 45 Minutes

Ingredients:

- 2 Whole peach
- 4 Ounce whiskey
- 2 Cup sugar
- 4 Tablespoon pink peppercorns
- 20 Whole fresh mint leaves, plus more for garnish
- 2 lime wedge, for garnish
- 4 Ounce bourbon

Directions:

1. For the Grilled Whiskey Peaches: cut peach into slices, then soak peach slices in whiskey in the refrigerator for 4 to 6 hours.

2. For the Pink Peppercorn Simple Syrup: In a shallow pan, combine sugar, 1 cup water and pink peppercorns.

3. Supply your smoker with wood pellets and follow the start-up procedure. Preheat the grill, with the lid closed, to 180° F.

4. Cook syrup down on the grill for 30 minutes, or until desired smoke flavor has been reached. Remove from the grill. Grill: 180 ˚F

5. Increase Traeger temperature to 350˚F and preheat. Place the whiskey peach slices directly on the grill grate and cook 10 to 12 minutes or until peaches soften and get grill marks. Grill: 350 ˚F

6. To make the Julep: Muddle 1/2 ounce Pink Peppercorn Simple Syrup with 10 fresh mint leaves and 4 slices of grilled whiskey peaches.

7. Add crushed ice over the rim of the glass. Pour bourbon over the crushed ice and stir. Garnish with 1 large sprig of mint and fresh lime. Enjoy!

Traeger Paloma Cocktail

Servings: 2

Cooking Time: 25 Minutes

Ingredients:

- 4 grapefruit, halved
- Smoked Simple Syrup
- 10 Stick cinnamon
- 3 Ounce reposado tequila
- 1 Ounce lime juice
- 1 Ounce Smoked Simple Syrup
- grilled lime, for garnish
- cinnamon stick, for garnish

Directions:

1. Supply your smoker with wood pellets and follow the start-up procedure. Preheat the grill, with the lid closed, to 350° F.

2. Grilled Grapefruit Juice: Cut 2 grapefruits in half. Place a cinnamon stick in each grapefruit half and glaze with Traeger Smoked Simple Syrup. Place on grill grate and cook for 20 minutes or until edges start to burn and it

acquires grill marks. Remove from heat and let cool. Grill: 350 ˚F

3. After grapefruits have cooled, squeeze and strain juice. It should yield 10 to 12 ounces of juice.

4. In a mixing glass, add tequila, lime juice, Traeger Smoked Simple Syrup and 2 ounces of the grilled grapefruit juice.

5. Add ice and shake. Strain over ice in an old fashioned glass.

6. Add a grilled lime slice and cinnamon stick to garnish. Enjoy!

Grilled Peach Sour Cocktail

Servings: 2

Cooking Time: 15 Minutes

Ingredients:

- 2 peach, sliced
- 2 Tablespoon sugar
- 1 1/2 Ounce Smoked Simple Syrup
- 4 Ounce bourbon
- 6 Dash Bitters Lab Apricot Vanilla Bitters
- 2 Sprig fresh thyme, for garnish

Directions:

1. Supply your smoker with wood pellets and follow the start-up procedure. Preheat the grill, with the lid closed, to 325° F.

2. Toss peach slices with granulated sugar and place directly on grill grate. Cook for 20 minutes or until grill marks form. Remove from grill and let cool. Grill: 325 ˚F

3. Place peaches and Traeger Smoked Simple Syrup into tin and muddle. Peaches should form about an ounce of juice during the muddling. Once completed, add remaining ingredients and shake.

4. Pour contents into glass over fresh ice and garnish with fresh thyme. Enjoy!

Grilled Hawaiian Sour

Servings: 2

Cooking Time: 15 Minutes

Ingredients:

- 2 Whole pineapple, trimmed and sliced
- 1/2 Cup palm sugar
- 3 Ounce bourbon
- 2 Ounce grilled pineapple juice
- 2 Ounce Smoked Simple Syrup
- 10 Ounce lemon juice
- 2 grilled pineapple chunk, for garnish
- 2 pineapple leaf, for garnish

Directions:

1. Supply your smoker with wood pellets and follow the start-up procedure. Preheat the grill, with the lid closed, to 350° F.

2. For the Grilled Pineapple Juice: Dust pineapple slices with palm sugar. Place directly on the grill grate and cook for 8 minutes per side. Grill: 350 ˚F

3. Remove from grill and let cool. Reserve a few pieces for garnish. Run remaining pineapple pieces through centrifugal juicer to extract juice.

4. To Make the Drink: Add bourbon, grilled pineapple juice, simple syrup and lemon juice to a cocktail strainer with ice. Shake vigorously. Double strain into a chilled coupe glass. Garnish with grilled pineapple chunk and pineapple leaf. Enjoy!

Smoked Mulled Wine

Servings: 10

Cooking Time: 60 Minutes

Ingredients:

- 2 Bottle red wine
- 1/2 Cup whiskey
- 1/2 Cup white rum
- 1/2 Cup honey
- 1 cinnamon stick
- 2 pods star anise
- 4 whole cloves
- 1 (3 in) orange peel

Directions:

1. Supply your smoker with wood pellets and follow the start-up procedure. Preheat the grill, with the lid closed, to 180° F.

2. In a shallow baking dish, combine wine, whiskey, rum, honey, cinnamon stick, star anise, cloves and orange peel. Stir well until combined.

3. Place the dish directly on the grill grate and smoke for one hour until the mixture is warm. Grill: 180 ˚F

4. Remove from grill and ladle into mugs leaving the mulling spices behind. Garnish with fresh cinnamon sticks, anise, orange zest or a combination. Enjoy!